THE
SPIRIT-FILLED
WORKING
WOMAN

THE
SPIRIT-FILLED
WORKING
WOMAN

52 Reflections to Guide and Inspire

SUE FUNK

credo
house publishers

To my hard-working daughter, Djanedi,

who inspires and amazes me with her love for others

and her energy and enthusiasm for life.

Contents

Introduction

THIS BOOK AND its themed weekly messages are dedicated to today's Christian working women. If you consider yourself as falling into this category—it does not matter what your profession or status—these thoughts are for you. This is a women's book written from a women's perspective with messages specifically geared to women. It is my hope and prayer that these thoughts will in some way be a comfort to you and a guide through your working career.

Life today is more complex and hectic than it was fifty years ago. Careers are open today to all women. This is as it should be, but you and I know that there are still barriers and some degree of unfairness that need to be overcome. We must encourage all young women to succeed. All young women need to get as much education as they can. They need to look ahead. They need to use their brains, organizational abilities, and any skills they possess to become prepared and to achieve success in a career. The reasons for this are as old as womankind. Women may find that they have been forced into a career because the partner they chose has unexpectedly died or decided to move on and has left them with children who must be fed and clothed. Women who planned to avoid working outside the home may find that the funds and assets they counted on for income have dried up, so that they are faced with the necessity of finding a job despite only limited education and skills. And the list could go on and on. There are no situations that are totally without risk, and today's young woman should prepare.

I chose one career, worked at it for a number of years, became bored, and decided to change course. I wanted a family and children, but I also knew that I wanted and needed a career. I loved to work and also loved my husband and child. I was lucky. I was able to have both family and career. However, it was not easy. I observed and experienced many challenges. My experiences and those of friends and co-workers have prompted me to write these devotionals. I know how busy working women are, so I have designed the messages to be read on a weekly basis, with each delineating a challenge to work on during the week. I hope they will be useful and encouraging for you. I am merely a layperson, but I have 45 years of experience in professional careers. I certainly made mistakes and am not perfect, but I hope these thoughts will help you through any struggles you may face. As I look backward—and ahead—I know that faith and Scripture provide all the answers. Sometimes the answer is hard to accept, but if it is clearly based on what Scripture teaches, you may accept it as true and reliable. We just need to open our minds and hearts through prayer, a focus on Scripture, and seeking the Lord. All things will be possible for you, and you may be assured that you will not be alone; you will have at your disposal the strength and power of the Holy Spirit to work through all challenges.

THE SPIRIT-FILLED WORKING WOMAN

Never Alone

THE BIBLE, particularly in Proverbs 31:10–31, celebrates the clever woman who can engage in commerce, manage a variety of activities, and still be the nurturer of the next generation. Most of you working women who will read this are doing all of this—and more—today. Over the next few weeks you will learn a lot about these women in the Bible.

You and your roles are vital. You are important. More importantly, you are loved by the Lord, and there are many ways for you to "do it all" with His help and support. In fact, if you let Him guide you and walk with you, this will be the most important help you can get, not only to survive in this hectic world but to truly succeed.

I hope these words of encouragement each week will be of some help as you face the pressures of work each day. I was a professional working woman for nearly fifty years before I finally retired and had to face new learning experiences like the challenge of staying at home and finding engaging tasks with which to occupy myself. That is another story for another time. For now, I want to share some encouragement from what I have experienced as a professional working woman and mom.

I experienced the many and varied challenges of the 21st-century office. There will be some who worked with me and knew me well who will be surprised by this book. I was not perfect. I made mistakes. I regret many decisions and actions I wish I could redo. However, I knew then, and I certainly know now as I look back, that I was infused with a spiritual presence and supplied with supernatural help through the rough times. How I wish I had been more faithful and that I had avoided some courses of action I willingly undertook due to my stubborn pride and refusal to listen to that still, small voice that often spoke to me. I know that I, as a Christian, was not alone on my journey and that I was often rescued from myself and my constant drive to succeed by the Holy Spirit, who was available to, with, and within me.

Friend, fellow working woman, I wish you well. I hope you may find some peace and guidance for those common office encounters and achieve more success than I ever did in overcoming the many challenges and temptations that are out there. I hope you will be more faithful in your Christian walk than I was. I am nothing more than a layperson who just wants to share some honest experiences that you may also be experiencing and to offer some words that might help you through the rough patches. I am not an expert but a fellow worker who has had a long history in dealing with the common, everyday working challenges.

Working women do not have a lot of extra time, but hopefully you will find a few minutes each week to read a devotional message designed to encourage you in your profession and help you cope with situations that arise in the office. It is my fervent hope and prayer that these reflections will speak to your heart and soul and help you realize that you are not alone—that there is a mighty God who truly cares for you more than you will ever realize. He is all-powerful, and there is no situation too difficult for Him to handle. Let Him share your load.

In Jesus' words in Matthew 11:28–30, "'Come to me, all you who are weary and burdened, and I will give you rest. Take my yoke upon you and learn from me, for I am gentle and humble in heart, and you will find rest for your souls. For my yoke is easy and my burden is light.'" Jesus knows and understands each and every challenge facing you, so let Him share your load.

Reflections

_____

_____

_____

_____

Going All In

ALL WOMEN WORK in one way or another. Why address these devotionals to one particular group? Fair question. I was a professional working woman for over 45 years. Many times I was made to feel guilty over my choice to work outside the home. This should not have been, nor is this perspective particularly biblical. My purpose is not to start a debate or to negate the importance of the woman who chooses or is able to stay at home as a wife and mother but to encourage those women in the working world who either voluntarily opt for a career or find it necessary to work outside the home to provide for their family. For all of us, the desire of our heart should be to walk with the Lord in all we do and show His influence in our lives to others.

The Bible is full of stories about strong working women. In Judges 4 and 5 you can read the inspiriting story of a woman, Deborah, who was a judge, a prophetess, a military leader, and an inspiring poet, along with a snippet from the life of a relatively unknown woman, Jael, who destroyed the leader of the enemy camp through cunning and skill. There are many other names we will encounter over the days to come, but the point is that wherever God has placed you, if there is work to do, tackle it with all your might (Ecclesiastes 9:10). Do not shrink from the tasks at hand. Do not feel guilty or ashamed that you cannot live up to some other person's ideal of who you should be or what you should do. Instead, ask daily for God to instill within you a sense of direction and to walk with you.

If you need inspiration, take a look once again at Proverbs 31:10–31. Some of you may recognize this familiar passage in part because it is often used at funerals. I say it should be the framed message given to every woman as she enters adulthood.

The passage does not condemn the working woman. Instead, it praises, validates, and declares her value. It reflects in remarkably contemporary terminology the many duties and activities of the active working woman, wife, and mother. With God's help she does it all. She buys and sells property, manufactures and trades, raises children and fulfills her role as a wife. She is industrious and ambitious, a provider and leader. The woman is successful, admired, and honored. There is no task she cannot perform. She is the pattern of the modern woman. She is you. You too are valuable and worthy of honor. Rejoice in your career and keep the Lord by your side. After all, he orchestrated these roles for you, and He will purposefully guide you.

Your challenge for the week is to not let anyone make you feel guilty or inferior because you are working outside the home or have chosen to pursue a career. Be grateful that the Creator God has plans to honor and prosper you if you let Him walk daily beside you. Be thankful to Him that He has given you the skills to work and honor Him by living so that others may come to know Him through you. Each day, allow this attitude and approach to be your mantra.

Reflections

_____

_____

_____

_____

_____

_____

No Fear

N THE WORKPLACE we often become fearful and uncertain. Someone may have said something harsh or demeaning to you. You may feel that there is a threat to your position. There may have been changes in management or in the direction of the company that cause you to question your abilities or status. New people may have been brought in who seem to be more popular with management. Your technical skills may not seem as strong as others'. Some with stronger personalities may denigrate and bully you or those around you. Doubt begins to creep into your mind, and doubt follows doubt. You begin to fear, to question, to be suspicious of your own abilities, . . . and you become depressed. You have trouble sleeping and relaxing. Your thoughts are constantly on the conversations and actions of others and what you perceive to be plots against you. You dread going in to work each day. Where do you turn?

One of my favorite verses of Scripture is aptly worded in the King James Version. In 2 Timothy 1:7 Paul reminds us, "For God hath not given us the spirit of fear; but of power, and of love, and of a sound mind." The NIV puts it this way: "For the Spirit God gave us does not make us timid, but gives us power, love and self-discipline." Think about this! With God's help we do not need to be afraid of any challenge or person! His power, which resides within all believers, enables us to face any challenge, person, or path with confidence. We don't have to let the office situations or other workers get us down. We have power—and it is God given!

First, notice that we are not given a spirit of fear. Fear will cripple us. It is senseless and unproductive. Satan loves to make us fearful. Your fears may run so deep that you are afraid that you will lose your job or be demoted. If you become fearful, you will react in a rash manner and can become to some degree functionally paralyzed. You will make mistakes. Slow down. Do not be afraid. Instead, prepare yourself. Start with prayer. Pray about the situation and for the person. Yes, pray for the very person causing you so much grief. Pray that the Holy Spirit will guide and protect you and that He will bind Satan away from you and the situation. Ask the Lord for help in determining which way to go, and then proceed confidently, with a clear mind and conscience.

Next, remember that you have a sound mind. You are not crazy, misguided, or lacking in knowledge. You have been trained and are competent in your job. You know how to judge a situation and assess what results are needed. Be clear minded, and quit fearing what someone else will say, how your actions will be perceived, or whether you will be liked. Let His love replace all your fears. Let His power fill you with confidence.

There is no need to state a challenge for this week. I am sure you see the path ahead plainly. Memorize these Scriptures, apply them to your life, and walk confidently without fear.

Reflections

_____

_____

_____

_____

_____

_____

His Plan and Provision

THERE IS NOTHING wrong with women having ambition and seeking success in the workplace. In fact, if you are going to work, or if you must work in the public arena, do it with enthusiasm and determination. Don't be afraid to step out and strive to achieve the highest status and level of success you can. If you have particular skills, hone them. Use them.

Some of you may have purposely determined that you want a career and intend to work in a chosen field. Others may have been forced into a career due to a variety of reasons that were beyond their control. It does not matter how you came to be a career woman, but it does matter how you approach your situation now. The majority of women have determined that they want a family and children as well as a career. There is nothing wrong with wanting it all. Most women today find that working in a career, in conjunction with taking care of a family, is expected, or at least normative and natural. Nothing has essentially changed in this regard since the beginning of time. Careers may have looked a little different hundreds or thousands of years ago, but women have always worked to add income to the household.

For a great number of centuries, depending on one's culture of origin, many professions did bar women, but all of that has changed, and the doors have for the most part been thrown open. I did not say that all avenues will be without problems, jealousies, discrimination, or challenges, but only that, for the most part, women can enter into any profession in most parts of the world. The point is that whatever work you choose to do, you can do it. It is easier, of course, to "do it" with help. Start with a right relationship with the Lord, and He will direct your paths and help you succeed in facing the daily challenges.

There are several verses of Scripture that should encourage everyone to have confidence, to realize that we are not alone or expected to make the journey in our own strength. Proverbs 3:5–6 reminds us that if we trust in the Lord with all our strength, He will guide our paths. As we journey from day to day, hopefully it will become clear to us how to more completely learn to trust Him and let Him guide us. One of my favorite verses, which I quote a lot, is Jeremiah 29:11: "'For I know the plans I have for you,' declares the LORD, 'plans to prosper you and not to harm you, plans to give you hope and a future.'" Just meditate on this verse. What a comforting thought that the God of the universe has plans for you and me. We are that important to God!

The challenge for this week is to reflect on your relationship to your Creator and to realize His deep love and concern for you and what you do. He personally knows you and is just waiting to guide you into the perfect place He has determined for you. Learn to trust Him.

Reflections

_____

_____

_____

_____

_____

_____

God's Words on Relationship

OW DO YOU perceive the Bible? You are an educated, modern woman. Do you see it as relevant to your life today? Unfortunately, many people fail to realize how important and foundational to your faith a daily reading of Scripture really is. In trainings on the job and in seminars we are taught the importance of relationships—of how to build them, how to succeed by networking, when to terminate unproductive affiliations, etc. It is all about relationships.

The Bible is about the greatest relationship of all. It is about your relationship to the God who created you and prepared a way for you to be in relationship with Himself. Unlike other relationships, the one with Him is eternal. If you build a relationship with Him, it will not be in danger of ending if you become old or ugly, gain weight, become unpopular with the cool crowd, or move to another location. It is for eternity. He does not care how you look or what your stock portfolio contains. Far from wanting anything from you, He stands ready to give you everything you need. The Scriptures are the path to developing that relationship with God. If you do not have a Bible, buy one or download one on your phone. There are many excellent translations. Just get started reading.

Let me call to your attention 2 Timothy 3:16–17: "All Scripture is God-breathed and is useful for teaching, rebuking, correcting and training in righteousness, so that the servant of God may be thoroughly equipped for every good work." As a servant of God, begin each day to read His Word, His message to you. If you are not familiar with the books of the Bible, perhaps you should start with one of the first three in the New Testament. You will find one of the best stories ever told in any one of these Gospels you choose, but more importantly you stand ready to begin a relationship with the author that will last an eternity. He inspired the Gospel writers to record these words, after all, with you in mind.

Reflections

_____

_____

_____

_____

_____

_____

_____

_____

{ 6 }

Perspectives and Priorities

WO THINGS THAT have struck me as I have gotten older are the fragile and temporary nature and uncertain duration of a person's life. Most all of the adult relatives and friends who were important to me in my childhood and who were alive fifty years ago are gone now. Within the next fifty years I and all of my present friends and relatives will have departed the scene. All of the issues, causes, and concerns we deem so important today will either have faded in importance or completely vanished except in the pages of history.

We all march step by sometimes tenuous step across a giant stage, with various and ever changing scenes flashing in the background to delineate our particular stage of life, but we are all headed for the stage exit. We will pass away as surely as have those who lived before us. Everyone and every generation, despite certain knowledge to the contrary, believes or at least lives as though they will be around forever. All of the present relationships you have been building at home, in the office, in the community, and in church will fade away. Only the eternal relationship you have established with God will last and remain important. First Timothy 6:7 puts it like this: "For we brought nothing into this world, and we can take nothing out of it."

Keep these thoughts in mind as you tackle your office chores each day. While it is important to do good, honest work, think of how much, or how little, of your legacy will still be pertinent fifty years from now. This is not to trivialize your work but to get you to think about the number of hours you spend at work in relation to what is really important in the eternal scheme of things. If you continue engaging 1 Timothy 6, keep reading through the verses that follow verse 7. If we put work and the pursuit of wealth ahead of righteousness, we may be falling into the trap of believing that wealth will bring us happiness. Verse 10 reminds us that "the love of money is a root of all kinds of evil."

While we must work, and work honestly and diligently, for our bread, we don't want work to become a substitute for the things that really matter. The daily work we do is temporary in terms of its influence and impact, and we need to take stock of what will really matter at the end of our life. I can tell you from personal experience that after a long career it has not been the work that I did but the relationships I have cultivated, the bonds I have made—with my Lord, my family, and my friends—that have had a lasting impact. This week, evaluate your available time to see whether you need to balance your work time with more attention to the eternal.

Reflections

_____

_____

_____

_____

_____

_____

Guarding Our Heart

N THE WORKPLACE there is nothing more important than keeping up with tasks. So it is with all other aspects of our lives. There are work tasks, home tasks, child-related tasks and activities, and our family and social obligations. What should be our priority? How do we do it all and keep our sanity? Some make lists. Others post reminders in their phones, in books, or on tablets, scrap paper, or chalk boards. For a few, mental notes are sufficient. There are so many things to do, so many activities to track. So how do we determine what is important? How do we prioritize in order to get to the place we need to be?

The same is true for the spiritual life. Where do we start in terms of our spiritual priorities? There is a helpful checklist found in Proverbs 4:23–27. With the help of this passage, we will look for guidance from its four suggestions over the next four weeks. As you begin each day of this week, focus on just the first suggestion in the checklist.

Proverbs 4:23 directs us to ask God to guard our "heart" or mind. Our heart is the essence of who we are—our core identity. It is the real person inside of you. How do you look at your boss? What do you really feel and think about her? What are your real thoughts about your fellow workers? How do you honestly feel about family and friends? Has your heart become hardened to them in some way? Have you "guarded" your heart from developing resentments against them? How do you show your love to them? Do your actions and thoughts reflect that love that Jesus taught us so much about? Do you pray for them?

The focus for you this week will be consideration of how we really feel in our hearts and minds—and how we might change those thoughts and feelings in a positive direction. Let your heart and thoughts be guided by His love. Push away any thoughts of jealousy, hatred, desire for revenge, pride, and selfishness, and replace these negative thoughts with ones that will elevate your walk with the Lord and promote a better working relationship with those around you. We are commanded over and over again in Scripture to love others. Sometimes this is hard, but we need to elevate this mandate to the number one spot in terms of our thoughts and intentions. Pray that your thoughts and actions each day will be guided by love, as well as for the power to love those with whom you do not agree or whom you feel have wronged you. Pray to love others as Jesus loved you. Pray that your heart may be guarded against all of the evil and temptations that are set before you.

This is a daunting task for just one week. Recall, though, that your heart and mind *are you*. You—relying on the Spirit's strength, of course—have the power to make yourself into the person you want to be and to influence how you will be perceived by others. Take the challenge in Proverbs, and work to guide your heart and mind toward the things of God and away from evil. Take note of what a difference this trajectory will make in developing in yourself a more spiritual and meaningful relationship with God. Wake up each day prayerfully asking Him to help you "guard" your heart throughout the day.

Reflections

_____

_____

_____

_____

_____

_____

Reining in the Tongue

AST WEEK WE began to reflect on a checklist based on Proverbs 4:23–27. The challenge was to begin each day asking God to guard our hearts or minds to love others. This week we look at the second item on the checklist. Proverbs 4:24 calls on each of us to "keep your mouth free of perversity; keep corrupt talk far from your lips." How many times per day does our tongue get us into trouble? Do we get into trouble because we say too much or because we speak too many unnecessary words? Isn't it better sometimes to just keep quiet and not comment at all? How much of our talking each day includes unhealthful words in the form of gossip, hurtful or discouraging comments, untruths or half-truths, tacky retorts, profanity, or disdain? It takes a lot of effort sometimes to just ignore comments made to you, to keep quiet and not respond to baiting or biting remarks. Proverbs 15:1 reminds us that "a gentle answer turns away wrath, but a harsh word stirs up anger." In any workplace there are the "spoons"—those individuals who stir the pot constantly. Learn to manage them by not letting them stir you to the point of saying something you will regret later.

The tongue is powerful and hard to control. Once something is spoken, it cannot be unsaid. Emotional harm from the spoken word can last a lifetime. In an office environment words spoken in haste may never be forgotten. It is better to think the situation through before you respond. I knew a very successful manager who would do his best to wait until the following day before responding to a situation. He knew that, whenever possible, he needed to choose his words carefully and be sure that he was not reacting emotionally but responding logically and fairly. When he did speak, people respected his decisions and listened. I suspect that he may have been familiar with James 1:19–20, in which James advises us to "be quick to listen, slow to speak and slow to become angry, because human anger does not produce the righteousness that God desires."

The challenge this week is to pray each day for power over our tongues. Add this to the list we are building from this passage in Proverbs. All of us can remember words spoken years ago that hurt us deeply. Words are powerful. What we say to each other reflects what is truly in our hearts and minds. This week, as you wake each day, ask God to guard your heart and mind, as well as to grant you power over your words.

Reflections

_____

_____

_____

_____

_____

_____

Fixing Our Eyes

CONTINUING WITH PROVERBS 4:23-27, this week we look at the third item on this checklist. Verse 25 calls on each of us to "let your eyes look straight ahead; fix your gaze directly before you." I know that there are varied interpretations to this verse and that it flows along within the context of the remaining verses in this chapter. In the workplace setting, it means that we are to keep our eyes focused on what is truly important and good—on the things that are necessary and productive, while letting the "little things" go. What is important at the end of the day—and at the end of our lives—will not be the recognition we have fought so hard to achieve. It will not be who won the battle over whatever issue or who was working hardest in the office. The conflicts over job assignments and promotions will have lost their relevance. How much time do you spend worrying about how you look, what people will think of your house or car, who makes the most money, or what it will take for you to get ahead of others? In fact, most of what we spend our time worrying about and focusing on will not be remembered at all. So much of our effort is spent on things that will not stand the test of time. They seem important at the moment, and we focus a lot of energy, time, and angst on them, but in the end they have neither relevance nor value.

So on what are we to focus? On what should our eyes be fixed? The most important things are those of the Spirit—the things that are eternal. We need to set our gaze on relationships that are meaningful and will last. What is our relationship with our spouse, children, family, and friends? If our gaze is regularly focused on how to get ahead of someone else, what material possessions we have or desire, our quest to become popular, or how we can make more money, we will lose sight of the issues and relationships that are eternal.

You cannot have a right focus here on earth unless you start with a right relationship with the eternal God. As Jesus enjoins us, we are to seek first the kingdom of heaven, resting assured that everything else we truly need will be provided. The way to begin that focus is to seek to know the One eternal God through His Son, Jesus. Scripture alone can guide you, and prayer alone can sustain you. The Bible presents God's plan, but if you do not already know and believe that Jesus is the culmination of that plan, talk to a minister or someone you know is a Christian; ask questions and let them guide you. Two Scriptures provide the answers you need to find Jesus: John 3:16 and Romans 10:9–10.

Your challenge this week is to identify and evaluate your life focus. Along with asking God each day to guard our hearts and minds and give us power over our tongues (issues addressed during the past two weeks), we now add our request that He will help us to first discover and then to fix our eyes—our focus—on what is truly important in life. This is quite an assignment for just one week, but my prayer for you is that this quest will take you on a journey of discovery about yourself and your career.

Reflections
_____

_____

_____

_____

_____

_____

_____

_____

Staying the Course

W E HAVE BEEN looking at Proverbs 4:23–27 at a checklist for how we should pray as we begin each day. To review, the writer suggests that we (1) ask God to guard our heart or mind; (2) ask for power over our tongue; and (3) pray to keep focused on what is really good and important in life. In addition (4), we will look this week at our need to remain on the right path, as described in verses 26–27. We need to ask Him to make the path straight and to keep our feet firmly on level ground. We are to ask Him to prevent us from wandering off to the right or left, to keep us from straying off the right path and to avoid evil.

What does this mean? We all want to go our own way. Most of us want to be in control, and we are accustomed to making decisions. After all, leadership ability, a desired attribute in the workplace, is highly sought after. If we have been blessed with natural leadership abilities, it is hard to surrender and let Him truly lead and guide us on the right paths to follow and toward the right decisions to make. How you handle situations in the office— whether, for example, you choose to exact revenge for some slight, determine to undermine someone else's chance at success, directly address an ethical dilemma, enjoy the activities of the gang after work, or boost your ego with a slight flirtation—all such decisions are determined by the path you have chosen to follow and by whom you are allowing to determine your path.

What it the right path to follow? We do have choices, and the purpose of letting the Lord direct our paths is to keep us from evil options. Evil lurks everywhere, waiting for us to veer to the left or right and get off the path He has chosen for us. Things out there, off the path, often look good and appealing. Temptation is real and powerful. In Matthew 7:13 Jesus taught, in effect, that both the gate and the path or road that lead to destruction are wide and enticing. That is why we need to give careful thought to the path we choose for our lives each day. Jesus also taught that the path of righteousness is narrow and warned that only a few will find it. We need to deliberately and consistently seek the narrow path.

This week, we conclude our checklist study. Our fourfold mission involves our need to pray each day for (1) a right heart and mind, (2) control over our tongue, (3) the ability to see and focus on what is truly good and important, and (4) for Him to direct our path and keep us from evil.

Reflections

_____

_____

_____

_____

_____

_____

_____

The Manual

I N EVERY PROFESSION there are manuals for guidance. There are personnel manuals, teaching manuals, technical manuals, directional manuals, legal manuals, computer manuals, procedural manuals, etc. Manuals contain a wealth of knowledge and represent hours and sometimes years of study by individuals and teams. The guidance provided in manuals is needed for accountability and success at all levels of business. Great planning, time, energy, and effort go into their production.

So it is with the Christian life. The Bible is our manual. God's Word is composed of many books and was compiled over many centuries. It is as relevant and real to us today as it was when written. It holds the answer to all of life's questions and situations, but in order for us to internalize those answers we must read and refer to it daily. The real author is God, and the individual books contain the divinely inspired word of the Creator, passed along to us by those He chose as His conduits to disseminate those words. Scripture is His primary method of communicating to the receptive heart.

As questions arise in your business or life situation, know that this wonderful resource contains His guidance and answers. People today face the same situations and experience the same temptations and moral dilemmas as those who lived in the centuries past. You cannot mention a problem or question the Bible fails to address. The answers are right there for any situation. Encouragement and insight in one form or another are seldom more than a page or two away. As Solomon declared centuries ago (see Ecclesiastes 1:9), there is nothing new under the sun that the wisdom of God cannot solve. Wisdom is tantamount to knowing God. The best way to learn about someone—or, more to the point, to get to know someone—is, after all, to read their book.

Just as you have your business manuals handy on your shelves or stored in a file on your computer, so you should have a reliable translation of the Bible stored on your phone or computer or handy in hard copy. Beyond simply having access for ready reference is the need to immerse yourself in Scripture by reading some each day. Jesus Himself quoted Scripture constantly and declared that every word will be fulfilled before the end of time. In Matthew 4:4 He tells us that humans live more by the Word of God than by bread. The Bible can provide a source of strength that will sustain you better than the words of any philosopher or philosophy of today. Begin to take advantage of God's direct power and strength by reading and searching His Word daily.

Your challenge this week is to take a few minutes each day to read a Bible passage. If you are not already on a daily plan to read through the Bible. I recommend that you choose one of the four Gospels at the beginning of the New Testament and begin reading. My hope is that you will become fascinated with the stories of Jesus and His ministry and find yourself compelled to continue reading each day.

Reflections

_____

_____

_____

_____

_____

_____

_____

_____

The Right Path

L ET'S THINK ABOUT the "new" year. All businesses have an anniversary or annual beginning—an opportunity for evaluation and course correction. A new fiscal year allows a reset for accounting, tax, and other purposes. It might be the actual New Year celebrated on January 1, or it might fall in June or some other month. No matter what the arrangement, this is a traditional time of new beginnings, new thinking, and new resolutions. How can this benefit you in your role as a working woman?

Take a serious look at yourself, and think back over the past year. Do you feel that you are in the right place? Sure, you will think of things you will want to improve as you make a fresh start, but ask yourself more basic, sweeping questions, like "Am I in the right job for me?" "Do I feel that what I am doing is what God wants me to do?" "Can I see myself doing this for the next five, ten, or twenty years?" If not, start searching for what and where He does want you to be. The Lord is for you and with you: He knows you intimately and has a blueprint and agenda for you. He wants you to walk with Him, so that you may prosper and grow, both spiritually and in many other ways. To return to a favorite verse of mine, the prophet Jeremiah 29:11 quotes the Lord as saying, "'For I know the plans I have for you, . . . plans to prosper you and not to harm you, plans to give you hope and a future.'" It is humbling to think that the God who created the universe and controls its ultimate destiny is ready to lead and sustain each of us individually. He knows us personally much better than we could ever know ourselves.

The very first step in determining God's plans for you is to be in a right relationship with Him. God had a plan from the beginning of creation to provide a path of salvation to all who would seek Him and follow His commands, and that path is through His Son, Jesus. As this New Year (whatever its date) begins, take time to evaluate your relationship with the One who truly knows you and your needs. Submit your life and heart to Jesus as a first step. As promised in Scripture, you will be given the power of the Holy Spirit to walk with you daily. Then turn over your plans and life to Him and seek His will for your life. You will be surprised at the doors that act of faith will open for you and the peace that will empower you to find solutions to your life and work you might never otherwise have thought possible. That is the journey I hope we will take together this year as we look at situations in the office and how to address them. No one can be successful in this journey without the power of the Holy Spirit within.

Your challenge this week is to devote some time each day to thinking about what you are doing and why. Pray each day and ask God to show you the path that is best for you, to open the door for you to wherever it is you should be doing. It may be that you are already in exactly the place He wants you to be; if so, pray to be fruitful there.

Reflections
_____

_____

_____

_____

_____

_____

_____

Realizing Your Potential

AMBITION: SHOULD a woman have it? Absolutely. Do you feel guilty because you are ambitious? You should not! The Bible does not command women to be weak. Let me take a very well known example as proof of what I am saying. Proverbs 31:10–31, which we have considered before, is a familiar passage that is often read at a woman's funeral. That application of the passage is very appropriate, but I advocate reading this to young women as they are starting out in life. If you read the passage carefully, you will see the profile of a very busy, accomplished woman who is involved in several businesses, real estate acquisition, supervision of employees, social and cultural activities, and teaching, while at the same time being careful not to neglect her children and household. If this isn't a description of the working woman of today, I don't know what is! Be inspired. Note that near the end of the passage the secret of her success is identified: she trusts in and fears the Lord. In the weeks to come we will explore the meaning of this secret power and how it continues to be a foundational requirement for success in today's world. This woman who is described in Proverbs lived over three thousand years ago, but you too can do any job or solve any problem you encounter, as long as you approach it with the Lord's help and guidance.

Your challenge this week is to refuse to let fear sidetrack or paralyze you and instead to act with confidence. Take stock of your talents and abilities. We are not all alike. If you have a particular skill, interest, or ability, develop it. Really take some time to evaluate yourself. You may honestly lack some skills that others have, but if you look closely at yourself you will recognize the skills and abilities God has given you that you can put to use. Ask the Lord to help you use what He has given to you to your fullest potential.

Reflections

_____

_____

_____

_____

_____

_____

_____

A Life-Transforming Adventure

THE BIBLE REVEALS God, His Son, and His plan for an eternal relationship with all of His creation—very much including you. To learn how to be in a right relationship with God, Bible reading is the key. If you are a believer already, do not neglect the privilege and opportunity you have to read the inspired Word of God. Try to engage with it daily. A young child who is starting to read and understand does not start with some work by an 18th- or 19th-century philosopher. The same applies to you: if Bible reading is not something you are already doing, start with the basics, such as the Gospels of Matthew, Mark, Luke, and John. Acts, the last of the four historical books that begin the New Testament, is an exciting account of early Church history and the works of the Holy Spirit as the gospel message was spread. It is action packed and captivating.

Genesis and Exodus, the opening two books of the Old Testament, launch the story of the Jews and their pivotal role in God's overarching plan. God chose the Jews as His people and assigned them to be the messengers, the conduit, to the world of His plan of salvation for the whole world. The Old Testament is full of promises that culminate in the coming of Jesus, His death, and His resurrection, all of which is recorded in the New Testament. The New Testament does not replace the Old but is a continuation of the revelation of God's plan for the world. Fortunately for us, God provided a way of salvation that was not only for His original chosen people, the Jews, but one that enabled all of humankind to come to know God through faith in His Son, Jesus the Messiah.

The apostle Paul gave some good advice to his protégé, Timothy. In 2 Timothy 3:16–17 he pointed out to this young evangelist that "all Scripture is God-breathed and is useful or teaching, rebuking, correcting and training in righteousness, so that the servant of God may be thoroughly equipped or every good work."

As your relationship with God grows, you will want to study His Word and promises and to understand His plan for the world. Studying the Scriptures will unlock a power and a presence that would otherwise have seemed unimaginable. It will be a life-transforming adventure that will bring you peace. Use the week ahead to begin to study the Bible daily.

Reflections

_____

_____

_____

_____

_____

_____

_____

_____

Watch Those Words

A S YOU RUSH into the office each day, what is the first thing you do (after getting that cup of coffee, of course)? Unfortunately, I must confess, I was always eager to hear the latest news, gossip, and rumors. Information is power, and I was just as eager as the next person to hear the latest and offer my opinion on the topic of the day.

A typical office, whether composed of two or twenty or more people, will reflect differences of opinion on any and every topic. There is usually something or someone to complain about. The complaints may be perfectly justified, but it is our choice whether to complain with the crowd or take a higher road. People in the office are watching the believer all the time. Your actions will, as is often said, be the only testimony—the only version of the Bible— some people will read for their entire life. How you respond is so important. Think before you throw more fuel onto that growing fire. If you do not join in, or if you stop complaining, it will be noticed. Your silence and determination not to chime in will be speaking more loudly than the words you would have offered to the controversy. To promote factions and frictions in an office, far from being a reflection of the Spirit, is actually prompted by our sinful nature. See Galatians 5:14–15. The command to love your neighbor as yourself is repeated here. I resonate with the direct warning in verse 15: "If you bite and devour each other, watch out or you will be destroyed by each other." Better not to become em- broiled in controversies that will all pass in time anyway.

Proverbs is full of so many sayings against gossip that it is hard to choose a representative verse, but 15:4 says it as well as any: "The soothing tongue is a tree of life, but a perverse tongue crushes the spirit." Again, Proverbs 19:9 reminds us that "a false witness will not go unpunished, and whoever pours out lies will perish." Enough said!

The challenge this week is to change your behavior that tends to get embroiled in gossip and backbiting. Challenge yourself by seeing how many days you can avoid gossiping and degrading comments behind someone else's back.

Reflections

_____

_____

_____

_____

_____

_____

_____

Stoking the Flame...or Stomping the Embers?

I N MATTHEW 5:1-12 there is a section in Jesus' well-known Sermon on the Mount we refer to as the Beatitudes. I encourage you to read this beautiful passage of Scripture. One of the most surprising and poignant statements appears in verse 9: "Blessed are the peacemakers: for they will be called the children of God."

What does this mean in the office environment? From the minute you get more than one person in an office, there will be differences of opinion, conflict, gossip, contention, and jealousies. You can be the person to contain the emotion and seek to maintain a professional atmosphere. You can kindly turn conversations away from gossip to more positive statements about the person or situation. You can be the person to refuse to pass the gossip along.

You can be the person to try to find a suitable middle ground or to persuade, logically and lovingly, to bring out the merits of a particular path. Although the final decision may not be yours to make, you do not have to be a willing party to opinions or decisions that conflict with your beliefs or compromise your values.

The flames of controversy are easily fanned, however, and can result in reducing a wholesome working environment to one of bitterness, meanness, and bitter toxicity. Watch what you say and how you react. After all, you work there, too. You want your career to succeed, and you certainly do not want to develop ulcers and dread going to work each day because of the conflicts and jealousies that exist there.

We talk a lot about peace. We hope for peace on earth and goodwill to all people, as we so readily, and perhaps blithely, declare during Christmas. But what about every day? The peace *around* us in large part depends *on* us. In Paul's words in Romans

THE SPIRIT-FILLED WORKING WOMAN

12:18, "If it is possible, as far as it depends on you, live at peace with everyone." This puts the burden squarely on each of us to seek ways to promote peace in the office, and that is going to require an active, involved, and intentional mind and heart. The role of the peacemaker is not a passive one. Each situation will call for effort and a lot of prayer for discernment and wisdom.

Let your challenge for the week to be to assume the role of the peacemaker. Be sensitive to situations that can quickly become contentious, and do what you can to turn the escalating dynamics into something positive. Christian woman, in order to be effective you must be active and filled with the Spirit through prayer and your own peaceful relationship with the Lord.

Reflections

_____

_____

_____

_____

_____

_____

_____

Counterintuitive Prayer

HERE IS AN old joke about being paranoid. It goes something like this: just because you think someone is out to get you doesn't mean that someone isn't out to get you.

Evil is out there, and no doubt Satan truly is out to get you in some way. Matthew 5:38–48 is a difficult passage to follow. It is even hard to read because it calls on us to do something that goes against our nature. It calls for us to truly take the high road by loving our enemies. I don't know about you, but my natural inclination is to take revenge or work on—or at least take pleasure in imagining—some scheme to get back at the person. Unfortunately, that approach is not what Jesus taught us to do.

Another passage of Scripture worth noting in this regard is Proverbs 25:21–22, which instructs us to be kind to our enemies. If your enemy needs something, so goes the injunction, give it to them. In doing so you will make them ashamed over what they have done to you. I love the phrase "you will heap burning coals on his head, and the LORD will reward you."

It is interesting that both the Old Testament and Jesus' own words in the New enjoin us to do good to our enemies. Jesus evens commands that we pray for them. Have you ever tried this? I will tell you that it is one of the hardest acts you will ever do. Do you have a particular feud with someone in your office or chain of command? Try praying for that person and for the situation that brought you into conflict. Maybe you feel that person is out to get you, does not appreciate the work you do or the role you play in the office, or is responsible for holding you back from what should rightfully be yours. If so, pray for the person. The first time will be the hardest. Yes, this anticipates that there will be a second and even a third time you will pray for this individual and for a removal of whatever barriers exist between you.

Your challenge this week is a hard one. Focus on the individual or individuals whom you feel would most like to destroy you. Then pray for them. Pray often. Observe how the situation between the two of you changes.

Reflections

_____

_____

_____

_____

_____

_____

_____

The Prodigal Within

WE HAVE ALL heard the story of the prodigal son, as found in Luke 15:11–31. This story contains numerous lessons at many levels. While most of us would argue that we have not run away from our family or responsibilities or entered into a carefree and wasteful cycle in our life, we have all strayed from the straight path from time to time. I suspect that there is a bit of the prodigal in each of us. One of the many messages implicit in the story is the way in which the father of the lost son welcomed him home when he returned. The father in the story is symbolic of our heavenly Father, who waits to welcome us back from our own wandering journey. There is no condemnation of the lost son, but only a joyous reception by the father.

There is another story, this one true, of a man who committed an infinitely more devastating and far-reaching sin than the prodigal son. Peter, despite his protests of loyalty to Jesus, denied knowing Jesus when He was on trial. Not only did he deny Him once, but he did so three times.

During the Last Supper Jesus tried to prepare His disciples for what was to come. No doubt the disciples did not fully comprehend the magnitude of the events that would take place in the next few days. Luke records an amazing statement by Jesus to Peter. In Luke 22:32 Jesus directed Peter that when he "turned back," he was to strengthen his brothers. Jesus knew that Peter would deny Him— and He knew the guilt and anguish Peter was going to experience in the aftermath of that unspeakable sin. Scripture records that Peter wept bitterly when he realized he had denied his Lord and Master. Jesus also knew that Peter would "turn back." Thankfully, we know the powerful force that Peter was in the early Church because he did turn back.

These two stories reveal to us that there is always a path back, no matter how far we have strayed from a right relationship with the Lord. The key in each story is that the person who has strayed must recognize what they have done and turn from the wrong path back to the right one. Once we have turned back we will be forgiven, and the Lord will restore us to fellowship with Himself.

Your challenge this week is to examine your path. Were there times when you were not on the right one or even determined in advance to go your own way, no matter the cost? If so, the way back is open, and the reunion will be joyous.

Reflections

_____

_____

_____

_____

_____

_____

_____

Workplace Fudging?

ET'S ASSUME WE are back at work after a day of celebrating one of our national holidays. We all feel refreshed, renewed, comfortable, and proud of our freedoms and the many things our country has accomplished. Is there any danger of our losing the freedoms and favor we have enjoyed as a nation? Most of us would dismiss the thought as an impossibility. We have existed and prospered for well over two hundred years, and there is absolutely nothing that can disrupt our progress in the direction of even greater things. We are still a "nation under God," and we are enlightened and tolerant and have only the noblest of intentions among the families of nations. God has obviously blessed us. There is no danger the Lord is going to abandon us . . . or is there?

With such obvious material wealth and power, is there any need for us to be concerned? Just as God's chosen people, the Jews, let impurities creep into their daily lives that slowly caused them to turn from God to following the corrupt practices of the nations around them, so we must be careful not to compromise our beliefs and allow corruption of all kinds to slowly turn us away from the Lord.

At work, the process might begin with our compromising our ethics. Everyone cheats a little on their taxes. It is good business to "make up" a little profit on one customer that you may have lost on another. The consumer will not know that the quality of a product has been compromised for profit. Have you heard fellow workers say any of the following? "The boss will not know if I take a small amount of cash." Or "The boss will not know I am searching the web or watching a movie behind my screen work." "No one will know that I occasionally look at a porn site from my station." "If I get the basic work done that is expected of me, what does it hurt if I take a little time for myself?" "I am not the only one doing this."

Sin begins and ends with a little thing we assume no one else will notice. The loss of God's favor begins in the same way. First Samuel 16:7 reads in part, "'The LORD does not look at the things people look at. People look at the outward appearance, but the LORD looks at the heart.'" The heart of our nation resides within each one of us and in a real sense *is* each one of us. Our nation is judged by the actions of each one of us and what we do and stand for. Let's not lose His favor individually, because this will open the door to our losing His favor collectively.

This week, examine the little allowances and negative habits that may have crept into your workday. Are you being totally honest with your time at work? Are you giving full measure to your boss and co-workers, or have you jiggled the scales a little because you feel no one else will notice or care?

Reflections

_____

_____

_____

_____

_____

_____

_____

_____

Team Players

LEADERSHIP. THERE MUST be leadership in an office, on a team, on a project, in the classroom, or to achieve a desired result. If there is more than one person in an office, one must take the lead. The role can go back and forth, but usually someone steps up to take charge. This is natural in the order of things. If that person possesses skills of organization, has an ability to motivate, is fair, and is a hard worker, things should go well. In the book of Judges we read about intermittent periods of weak leadership following the death of Joshua. Throughout the book the lament is reiterated that there was no king (leadership) and that everyone was doing what seemed right in their own eyes. This kind of moral relativity is the definition of chaos. A strong and righteous woman, Deborah, a respected judge, had to step up during one such period to help achieve order. Leadership is not limited to a particular gender but is demonstrated in one's natural abilities, willingness to accept responsibility and make decisions, and readiness to work hard without regard to self.

At work, if there is an absence of leadership for a project someone needs to step up with a plan. If this responsibility falls to you, or if you are the one willing to step up to the plate, research possible solutions and find a proper way to present your ideas, with the goal in mind of completing the project or task successfully and to your employer's benefit. If presented prayerfully and with a spirit of kindness, your plan should be accepted and you will be given a chance to demonstrate your abilities. If another's plan is chosen over yours, work to achieve it as you would have worked for your own. If another person's plan fails, you may have the opportunity to bring forward your ideas again. If one plan does not work, back up and try another. The path of progress is seldom a straight line. If you have leadership qualities, look for ways to present your ideas in a humble fashion. No one likes a steamroller. If you are self-aware enough to know that you do not possess leadership qualities, but know that you would make one darned good follower, look for ways to support and encourage the leaders, and then do your part to make the plans work. Good workers are always needed and appreciated.

Reflections

_____

_____

_____

_____

_____

_____

_____

_____

Futile Regret

I N MATTHEW 5:4 Jesus makes the counterintuitive statement that those who mourn shall be comforted. To mourn over something can take several forms. We naturally mourn the passing of someone we love. While this is expected and right, we need to find a way to move on and live with purpose and joy despite the loss. We need to be comforted. We also tend to mourn over past failures. Failure to work through and come to terms with past mistakes or sins in our life can wear us down. Too often we lament over and over again that we wish we had done something another way, chosen a different path, said something else instead of what we said, . . . and the list could go on and on.

To mourn incessantly over past situations and sins has a way of burdening us, of keeping us awake at night, of hanging like a dark cloud over our consciousness and limiting our ability to function efficiently and to relate positively with others. Only by approaching Jesus can we find our burden lifted and experience comfort. With any type of mourning we need peace—peace that will remove the clouds and lift the heavy burdens we are carrying. Many office conflicts result in sleepless nights and feelings of guilt. Whatever the situation or sin, Jesus invites us to take it to Him and leave the burden in His capable hands. "'Come to me,'" He invites in Matthew 11:28, "'all you who are weary and burdened, and I will give you rest.'" He will give you the peace only He can afford.

At another point Jesus asked an important rhetorical question: "'Can any one of you by worrying add a single hour to your life?'" (Matthew 6:27). To worry is to waste time and effort. It will not solve anything and will only cause you anxiety, loss of sleep, health problems, and possible mental or emotional illness. Instead, look for ways to increase your faith, turning to prayer and to a deeper reliance on the Holy Spirit to guide you. Jesus goes on to assure us that the heavenly Father knows what we need before we even ask. We are told to pray without ceasing and believe our prayers will be answered. After praying, we are to leave the issue—along with the outcome—to God's will, knowing that He will provide the answer in His time. As the Creator of all and with all power at His command, He has ultimate control of the situation. Trust Him and quit grieving over past regrets.

Reflections

_____

_____

_____

_____

_____

_____

_____

Improbable Virtue?

W HAT DOES IT mean to be meek? *Meek* is not a word used in everyday conversation. We don't think of meekness as a characteristic we might cite as a positive in a job description or resume. So why does Jesus declare in Matthew 5:5, "'Blessed [happy] are the meek, for they will inherit the earth'"? Wow! This makes a meek individual sound like someone who is particularly powerful and capable—and destined for great rewards! The truth is that, despite our culture's deprecation of meekness as weakness, meek people are teachable, wise, intelligent, and in possession of controlled, quiet strength. They are not out to trample others to gain recognition. They are confident and capable and know their bounds. They do not need to prove themselves but will work quietly and competently, often content to remain in the background. They are not reluctant to share praise with others because they are confident that their achievements will be recognized on their own merit. They are persons of noble character and ethics. The meek deliberately avoid the limelight. Look at your most dependable, capable co-worker or employee, and you will probably see a living representation of the definition of meekness. Are there lessons to be learned from the meek?

Your challenge this week is to assess your own qualities and develop those that demonstrate a degree of meekness. It doesn't work to say "Today, I will be meek." That would be something like saying "I am proud that I am so humble." So how do we develop the quality of meekness God so highly values? Meekness is summed up in self-control and the other spiritual qualities delineated by Paul in Galatians 5:22–23: "But the fruit of the Spirit is love, joy, peace, forbearance, kindness, goodness, faithfulness, gentleness and self-control. Against such things there is no law." The apostle adds in verse 26, "Let us not become conceited, provoking and envying each other."

If you take the challenge in Galatians 5 to develop the qualities that produce spiritual fruit, you will surely experience the promised blessings for meekness found in Matthew 5. The office or other job location is the perfect place to practice these virtues when dealing with co-workers or customers. Self-control when you are under pressure as you deal with incompetent, hostile, impatient, and rude employees, co-workers, and the public will develop within you great internal strengths. Leadership requires a calm, steady, measured response to all situations. Practice the fruits of the Spirit on all those you encounter this week. You will please some and confound those who would wish you ill, but you will see a difference in yourself and in your own degree of peace.

Reflections

_____

_____

_____

_____

_____

_____

_____

_____

23

Temptation and Its Antidote

THE OFFICE IS full of temptations, and temptations are the product of only one force. God does not tempt. No matter what you say or feel, that only leaves one other possible power—evil. Many people do not want to believe that evil or Satan exists. Scripture uses several titles, like the evil one, the devil, the power of darkness, demonic forces, demons, and the tempter, but all relate to Satan and his minions. Jesus made several references to him and included a petition in the Lord's Prayer that God would deliver us from evil. Satan is indeed real, and he and his demonic forces prowl about constantly looking for an opening in your life in order to worm their way in.

Jesus referred to the world as being under the influence of Satan, and in John 17 He prayed for strength for His followers in dealing with the trials and perils He knew we would encounter in the world. Satan is real, and his power is used to achieve evil. He is masterful at painting evil situations in pleasurable ways, and his goal is to drag you under his spell and move you as far away from God as he can. Ephesians 4:27 warns us not to give the devil a foothold, an opportunity to exert power over us. All persons are sinful by nature and therefore easily led into temptation. We need protection, and that means that we need to start with the basics. Do you know Jesus and believe that God sent Him into the world to provide a path of salvation for you? If not, the first steps are to claim the promise, believe in your heart, and confess with your mouth that Jesus is Lord. Read Romans 10:9–10.

The apostle Paul warned us that we are fighting against spiritual forces of evil, but we can rest secure in the knowledge that nothing can "separate us from the love of God that is in Christ Jesus our Lord" (Romans 8:39). We need the security and power that may be found only in our faith in Christ Jesus to be delivered from the temptations of the evil one that will come to all of us. No one is exempt from being tempted, but the power of the Holy Spirit is made available to every believer from the very moment they believe; you will have the power you need to withstand anything Satan might throw your way.

This week, make yourself aware of anything or any situation that would seek to move you away from God. Is it a tendency to put others down or to use profanity or gossip or engage in other conduct that you know could ultimately lead to sin? If so, realize that the world and its perspective have a ruler—none other than Satan. The power of the Holy Spirit is infinitely greater, but you must incorporate it into your life; though prayer you can invoke that power to protect you.

Reflections

_____

_____

_____

_____

_____

_____

_____

_____

24

The Slippery Slope

GENESIS 39 TELLS a riveting story that could have been written today and followed up with a movie version that would have soared on the charts. It is a universal story that is as true today as it was at time of writing. A handsome man and a natural leader with charismatic charm, Joseph was at his office doing his work diligently for his boss. The boss's wife pursued him with a passion. Her spoken intent was to have sex with him. Joseph refused her, tried to avoid any contact with her, and when he was inadvertently trapped in a room with her ran, leaving her holding his cloak in her hand. Joseph was a man of integrity and one who revered his relationship with God.

Joseph's example is simple enough—*run!* But, in today's work environment there is usually no place to run from the day-to-day encounters with sin in its various forms. A flirtation often starts innocently enough. Your co-worker, whom you see and must work with every day, begins to share with you how difficult his life is and how his spouse does not understand him. He hates to go home each day. He is miserable. He knows his troubles are not his fault. You become concerned. You empathize and express your hope that things will get better for him. He starts coming by your office more frequently, each time sharing more and more openly. He invites you to lunch to discuss his situation and get your input. Your friendship deepens. He wants more and more of your time and attention. Maybe you also find yourself in a rough spot with your spouse over finances, family issues, children, job pressures, travel requirements, health problems, or a myriad of other issues. So you listen. You, too, feel you are not to blame and that life has been unfair. So you begin to reciprocate by sharing your own troubles. You enjoy the distraction and attention. The door has been opened, and the dance begins.

While we want to help and encourage others, sometimes it is best just to take Joseph's cue and run. Watch for situations in which someone is trying to use you as a crutch instead of facing their issues directly. The slope is often a very gradual one that gets harder and harder to escape. Joseph had it right. Remove yourself as quickly as you can from a situation that will only grow more entangling. Stop and think of what it will mean to your life a year or two in the future if you continue along this path. Take your problems and issues to the One who can truly lead you through them. Encourage your co-worker to do the same, but make it clear that you are not the solution to his problems. Keep your distance emotionally and concentrate only on the work that you must do together.

This particular temptation is real, and it may well be one of the strongest you will ever face. Underestimating and yielding to it can cause you to lose a great deal in life. At stake may be your peace of mind, your present home life and relationships, your marriage, your children's lives and the impact the circumstances could have on them, your friendships, your job security, . . . and the list could go on and on. That is why it is so important to address such a temptation forcefully by fleeing from it. Paul's words in 1 Corinthians 10:13 apply here: "No temptation has overtaken you except what is common to mankind. And God is faithful; he will not let you be tempted beyond what you can bear. But when you are tempted, he will also provide a way out so that you can endure it."

As your challenge this week, identify some of the possible temptations around you. Get into a conversation with God and let Him help you either avoid them or find a way out.

Reflections

_____

_____

_____

_____

25

The Empathetic Approach

"I T MUST BE a full moon today." That is a familiar saying with
individuals who work with the public on a day-to-day basis.
It can seem as though the brighter the moon the more vocal the
customers, students and patients. Some days it is particularly hard
to put up with rudeness, profanity, unrealistic demands, and other
hurtful comments from people you are trying to serve and help.
Sometimes you just want to scream, "What part of 'no' do you not
understand?" Or "I really do not care! Tell it to someone else."

Yet we know we cannot respond that way. To begin with,
it would probably mean the loss of our job. Not to mention our
knowledge that we as Christians are called to a much higher standard of behavior. Once again the book of Proverbs provides some
guidance. For example, Proverbs 15:1 reminds us that "a gentle
answer turns away wrath, but a harsh word stirs up anger." I did
not say it would be easy, but it does work! In verse 18 of the same
chapter, we read that "the one who is patient calms a quarrel," and
in James 1:19 we are advised to "be quick to listen, slow to speak
and slow to become angry."

All of this is good advice to follow . . . but very hard to put into
practice on those days when it seems as though everyone with
whom you come into contact has a complaint or difficult request
or question. Too often we know the answer—and we know that
they are not going to like it. So we rush to speak rather than taking

a little time to listen patiently while they finish their tirade. A smile, a kind word, a compliment, an offer of alternative help, a glance directly into their eyes that conveys concern, or an acknowledgement that they do exist and matter may be the only gestures of kindness an upset person with a troubled spirit may receive. Wouldn't it be nice if the encouragement came from you?

Your challenge this week may not be easy, but it is straightforward: treat others as you want to be treated.

Reflections

_____

_____

_____

_____

_____

_____

_____

26

Worry Equity?

NOT TO BRAG, but I am an excellent worrier. I can take almost any situation and worry about it. I come from a long line of worriers, so I have learned from the best! My daughter says I can even create unimaginable scenarios to cause me angst. I am afraid this is true.

I found a gem of a passage in Matthew 6:25–34, though, and began to study and reflect on it. First of all, I reminded myself, this is Jesus speaking, and He makes His point plainly and simply: God, our heavenly Father, knows the things we need. He provides. Worrying will not add a minute to your life, and too much worry may definitely shorten it. Jesus instructs us in this beautiful passage to seek a close relationship with God, lead the style of life He would approve, and trust Him to provide whatever we need.

It is easy to become concerned about events and people at work, take the issues home with us mentally and emotionally, and stew over them, unproductive as this may be. A bad day at work often equates to a miserable evening with the family and a restless night for us. Leave the issues at the workplace. Do not continue to worry at home. Worry cannot change the events that have already happened. Tomorrow is a new day with a new opportunity to address a previous wrong or correct an erroneous situation. Resolve to use tomorrow for a fresh start with a new plan, and quit worrying over past events. Pray over the matter and ask for guidance in your approach and speech to others. Ask for a good plan that will reflect God's will and for a clear mind and spirit as you approach the opportunities inherent in a new day. Turn over the situation to the Lord and trust in His leadership. Your reward will be everything you need to make it through—and possibly even to triumph! Your challenge this week is to test this advice. Test your willingness to pray about the situation, put the matter in God's hands, and trust Him to take the lead and provide a path and direction through the issues you cannot resolve by worrying.

Reflections

_____

_____

_____

_____

_____

_____

_____

27

Working for What?

WHY ARE YOU working? What do you expect to get from working? Most of us would cite benefits like an income, satisfaction in helping others, something to do with our time, building a retirement income, or providing for our family. These are good reasons. No one can argue against them from the earthly perspective, but how long will any of these benefits last? There are other and less noble reasons for working that include the desire for power, influence, recognition, and just being able to buy more stuff. In Matthew 6:19–21, 33 Jesus gives us some guidance on where we should focus our efforts.

While it is true and good that we work to provide for our basic needs, we need to also work to store up benefits for our eternal existence. Jesus made it clear that the treasures we store up here on earth are vulnerable and temporary. If we store up heavenly treasure, on the other hand, it will secure for us an eternal reward. Jesus was saying that our efforts should be for so much more than obtaining monetary security, influence, power, or prestige, all of which are fleeting. Keeping a right relationship with God and putting Him as the number one priority in our lives is preferable— infinitely so!—and will result in rewards from God that cannot be lost and will provide all our needs on a permanent basis.

Since I have entered retirement, several things have become much clearer to me. I was one who put my work and career ahead of my family on many occasions. I could not imagine the office continuing to function without me and my exceptional abilities. Funny thing, but that office has done just fine without me for several years now. I foresee it thriving in the future as well. I also see that life is temporary. As a student of history, I have been impressed with the lives of great leaders of the past. All people walk across the stage of life one time. We play out our roles, but none of those roles lasts forever here in this world. We all have a little expiration date attached invisibly to us as we enter the world, and when our time is up, it is up. When you are young, you assume, at least on a feeling level, that your time will last forever. The truth is that this time is for your generation, . . . which will be followed by another.

What happens when this worldly life is over? A new life begins in the final phase of the eternity that began long before our births. Eternity already resides in all of us, and our preparation time for its ultimate phase is now. That is what Jesus meant when he directed us to store up treasures in heaven. Let your challenge this week be to evaluate where your treasures are and what it is you are storing up as you go out and work each day.

Reflections

_____

_____

_____

_____

_____

_____

_____

28

The Intensity Scale

HOW STRONG ARE you? Are you easily influenced by those around you? How do you evaluate yourself in terms of strength of character and beliefs? What drives you each day? In business you run into all types of people. You may be an employee of someone who places wealth as the top priority of their own life and of the business. You may have bosses or co-workers who perceive that the only way to get ahead is to make all the money they can as fast as they can and in any way they can. Do they influence you?

All businesses exist to make money—to realize a profit. This is the very definition of business. Employees are called to work for the good of the company and to promote and support the stated mission of the business. A good worker should go to work each day with the company goals in mind and return to their employer a good day's work in return for a fair wage and benefits.

However, if the love and pursuit of money begin to override all other considerations, disaster will happen. As Paul warns Timothy in 1 Timothy 6:10, "For the love of money is a root of all kinds of evil. Some people, eager for money, have wandered from the faith and pierced themselves with many griefs." Note that Paul cites the "love of money," not money itself. The intensity of our pursuit of profit and money is the issue. We all want to prosper, but if your pursuit becomes an addiction you will lose focus on what really matters in your life. Like any addiction, you become the slave and it takes over as the master.

Those who acquire wealth have received a wonderful gift, but one that is easily tarnished or lost due to arrogance, damage, theft, or greed for more. The danger for wealthy individuals is that they can become proud of their own accomplishments and feel as though they do not need God or anyone else. As with any gift God has given to an individual, it is expected that the gift of wealth will be used appropriately in service and obedience to God's commands. Some who have become wealthy have become corrupted by their own perceived ability to produce wealth. In effect, they have become their own god. Their dependence on God is replaced by self-assurance based on their own presumed ability to provide for themselves. Instead of displaying love for others as God has loved them, they become acquisitive and want even more and more of the world's goods. Unfortunately, too often they feel as though the normal rules of society do not apply to them and that they can buy their way out of any situation; the end, in the minds of many, justifies the means.

If you are an employee of such a person, you must guard your own desires. Do not let their addiction become your own. Be careful not to be corrupted by them and their focus on affluence. Life—the eternal life that is already our own—is more than money and what it can buy. It may be necessary or wise to continue being employed by this person, but it may under those circumstances be a particular challenge to place God first in your priorities. In 1 Timothy 6:17 Paul reminds us that wealth is uncertain and that our hope should be in God, who provides us with everything. Those who experience prosperity, and that would include almost all of us, should be generous and willing to share in order to store up treasure where it truly matters. Let it be your focus this week to evaluate where you are on the "intensity scale" in terms of seeking wealth.

Reflections

_____

_____

_____

_____

_____

29

Never Alone

FOR MANY OF YOU right now, time may seem to be crawling along. You struggle each day with children's schedules, lunches, after school sports activities, deadlines at work, projects that never seem to end or need constant revisions, impatient bosses, and co-workers' demands. Yet before you know it the years will have rushed by, and you will find yourself in another phase of life. Life itself really never slows down, but its pace and focus do change. Pressure of one type or another will always be with us. So no matter where you find yourself on the spectrum, take some time for yourself and get some spiritual help.

Carve out some space each day for a quiet time between yourself and the Lord. It does not have to be a long period of time, but it should be regular. Read some Scripture, pray, and just sit back and reflect on the positive aspects of your life. Evaluate your goals. Once you have prayerfully identified the issues that are troubling you, leave them with Him. Try to avoid revisiting the mundane issues and pressures that are taking up so much of your time and energy. Use this special time to call upon the Holy Spirit to fill your thoughts and actions with strength, clarity, and peace and to guide you through those issues you have confessed in prayer as troubling to you. As a child of God, you have the unlimited power of the Creator of the universe at your disposal. At work, you would never hesitate to use any and all resources available to you to accomplish the task at hand. As a Christian, your resources are prayer, Scripture, and the power of the Holy Spirit, who will take up those issues and guide you through them. In time, you will find that the best co-worker you have, the One who will consistently share in your work and life, is there beside you in the form of the Holy Spirit.

Jesus promised His disciples that they would not be alone in their struggles. As His follower, you, too, have the promise of John 14:16–17: "'I will ask the Father, and he will give you another advocate to help you and be with you forever—the Spirit of truth.'" We are not alone in any struggle we face. Our challenge is to use the resources available to us. Because we live in a fast-paced worldly society, we tend to overlook the power of the Spirit dwelling within us. A quiet time set aside each day can produce powerful results as you let the Holy Spirit take away your worries and concerns in exchange for His peace.

Reflections

_____

_____

_____

_____

_____

_____

_____

_____

30

Workplace Discrimination

N THE WORKPLACE there is no room for discrimination (in the sense of bias) of any kind. A person who is the victim of discrimination cannot and will not be able to do their best work. There are so many types of prejudicial treatment that can and will affect a person's job performance, to say nothing of how such negativity will impact their lives. At its root the word *discrimination* means distinction or the ability to distinguish, and the only discrimination (in the sense of discernment) that should be allowed is fair and honest evaluation of the output of all employees. If the work product is found to be substandard, there should be a serious and kindly executed effort to better train the individual. The evaluation should not be a personal attack, but one aimed at keeping productivity at an acceptable level.

Discrimination in its negative sense of favoritism can come in many forms: old-timers vs. new employees, age vs. youth, men vs. women, natural citizens vs. immigrants, rich vs. poor, to name a few, or it can be based on factors such as race, religion, sexual orientation, disability, social standing, or political beliefs. None of these factors is a legitimate basis on which to judge others in the workplace, and it is never permissible to harass or belittle anyone in any way. The focus should be on the job at hand, as well as on getting along together. Christian employees should not participate in any attempts to single out individuals for second-class treatment; each should be treated as they would treat their best friend in the office. In Colossians 3:8–11 Paul instructed believers to put away any anger, malice, and slander (as well as other negative conduct) from their lives. If negative treatment is directed at individuals simply because they fall into some category different from our own, these behaviors are wrong for a Christian to practice, not to mention counterproductive to the goal of a healthy working environment. Christians are to love as Jesus does, so that unbelievers may see God revealed in their actions. God will judge all actions and choices, but our command is to love. Paul states that because of Christ all people are equal. There is no longer any "status" to be considered, because we are all siblings in Christ and share equally in His grace and glory. In verses 12–14 of the same chapter, the apostle calls for compassion, kindness, humility, gentleness, and patience. If someone has wronged us, we are to forgive. If you love, truly love, as God through His Son has loved you, you will not judge someone else by any external standard. Instead, you will treat those with whom you work in a fair manner, with the goal of helping them do a good job, be successful, and enjoy working. Practice on your fellow employees some love, equality and kindness today and throughout the week and see what a difference it can make in your lives.

Reflections

_____

_____

_____

_____

_____

_____

31

Beyond Shelf Life

NO MATTER WHAT your business field, from time to time your office will experience a visit from some prominent person or may sign you up for a motivational seminar or training session. The speaker may be a titan in the field of business, a wealthy and powerful tycoon, a powerful political person, or a well-respected writer or public motivator. Whoever it is, they are someone of influence. We respect success and power and are eager to learn from someone who has accomplished notable things. Our response is a natural human reaction.

If we can learn from powerful and successful people, we may be able to achieve something along the line of what they have done. So we reach out, listen, envy, emulate, and hold them in respect for what they have accomplished. Yet we fail to realize how limited their influence and power really are. In time their favor will diminish; the riches and fame will disappear; and a fortunate few may be remembered as footnotes in history.

I recall one October day when I happened to be standing in line in one of the Disney parks. Someone walked by dressed as Elvis, and we commented on what a great costume it was. An adolescent boy in front of me turned and asked, "Who is Elvis?" Seriously? This encounter made me realize that even the most influential and talented of any generation has a shelf life.

How strange that we are eager to seek after powerful men and women but do not seek after the infinitely powerful Creator of the universe, the One who truly holds all power, riches, wisdom, and control. We ignore and discount the might of God, failing to recognize that He has written a book that has stood the test not just of generations but of millennia of people who have read it, been forever changed by it, and followed His teachings. We fail to acknowledge that He owns everything! Our very life, breath, hopes, and dreams belong to Him. Life is indeed meaningless and futile without Him. Yet instead we run after the latest fad, popular fashion, trendy philosophy, or charismatic leader. We eagerly buy into what they are selling and rush to proclaim them as our new god.

We need to rediscover the One true God who has a plan for every person's life. He alone has the answer for those seeking something to believe in and who desire eternal riches and assurance. His plan is marvelous in its design and implementation. He chose a people for His own, mandating them to make a way for all nations to come to know Him and receive His power. He gave His people rules and a book to guide them. Through this small group He brought His only Son into the world as a gift to humanity and offered all people the chance to become part of His family through faith in that Son. He provided unlimited access to His power through the gift of the Holy Spirit, who dwells within the heart of every believer to be with us through any test, trial, or challenge life can throw at us. This power is complete, eternal, not subject to a shelf life, and available at no cost. No one else but the One who created you can provide the security and wealth of eternal life. Seek Him, and all other good things shall be given to you through His power.

Reflections

_____

_____

_____

_____

_____

_____

_____

32

What We Owe Our Employer

DEPENDING ON HOW long you have been working and how old you are, you may remember some forms of employee treatment that are unheard of today—thank the Lord! I was having coffee with a group from our church, and we got to talking about some of the things we had experienced in the various workplaces represented by the group.

It is always important to dress for business. If you are in a profession that requires court appearances or meetings with the public, there is a certain level of dress that is expected and appropriate. To dress for success is not an empty mantra. It is still today expected that an athletic coach, a nurse, or a lawyer will dress differently from each other as they leave their homes to go to work. However, there was a time when women teachers were not permitted to wear slacks. They were required to work in dresses and appropriate hosiery. Administrations around the country finally relented and allowed coordinated, dressy pantsuits.

Also, if you as a teacher were to have become pregnant, you were required to resign or, depending on the expected time of delivery, your contract for the next year would not be renewed. It was assumed that it would affect the students negatively to see a pregnant teacher.

I remember that my husband and I, both teachers at the time, were counseled on proper after school activities—an area of life nearly all workers today would deem to be beyond the jurisdiction of the employer. We were cautioned that we must not be seen at any establishment that would be considered a bar, could certainly not be seen consuming alcohol, should not purchase alcohol publicly, and should not be seen doing anything that might provoke gossip in the community. Basically, we were told not to do anything that would bring unnecessary attention to our lives. It is easy to imagine how intrusive such rigid standards would feel in our personal lives today.

I mention some of these rather outlandish rules to make the point that one of the things any new employee should do is determine the "sacred cows" of the employer. Every employer or supervisor has certain rules they consider very important, and they are on the lookout for violators. It may be something to do with dress, where to park your car, how to address students in the hallways, or the expectation to help monitor the halls during class changes. If you honor the sacred cow rules, you will find your life at work more peaceful. If you feel the rules are particularly ridiculous and push against them frequently to make a point, you will likely find your job satisfaction to be less than what you want it to be.

So what do we owe our employer while at the workplace (even if we do not like all the rules)? Fortunately, there are many Scriptures that can provide guidance. Let's start with a principle set forth by Jesus when He was asked whether it was right to pay taxes to Caesar. As recorded in Matthew 22:21, Jesus said, "'Give back to Caesar what is Caesar's, and to God what is God's.'" That verse applies to our working life. While you are at work, your diligence, skills, and time belong to your employer. Yes, you need to follow the rules, no matter how frustrating or pointless. The employer, your personal "Caesar," and has chosen the image they wish to promote to the public.

As Christians, we are on display at all times with the example of Christ in our lives. There are many Scriptures that exhort us to work hard to bring profit and honor to our employer. We are to do an honest day's work for our pay. In honoring our employer, we honor the Lord.

Let your challenge this week be to follow Paul's advice in Colossians 3:23: "Whatever you do, work at it with all your heart, as working for the Lord, not for human masters."

Reflections

_____

_____

_____

33

Love in Action

WHAT KIND OF a co-worker are you? How do others see you each day? Would you like to improve your relationship with your fellow workers? Let's look at a very familiar passage in 1 Corinthians 13:4–8a. I am not a Hebrew or Greek scholar. I have been told, though, that the Greek word for "love" is a verb. Love is not just a feeling or emotion that is associated with affection, infatuation, or passion. It is active in its manifestation, necessitating follow through in action and attitude.

Paul states in verse 4, "Love is patient, love is kind. It does not envy, it does not boast, it is not proud." Applying these standards to us in the workplace today, there is a lot to unpack in this one verse. If you are a supervisor or team leader, I suspect that patience is one virtue you find difficult to master. Most of us type-As want the project finished. We want everyone to be focused and on target. The bottom line is always on our minds. It is hard to be patient, let alone kind at the same time.

Envy. Oh, my. If you are working on developing patience and kindness, it may seem almost too much to ask yourself at the same time to control your feelings of envy. The biblical writer James warns us in chapter 3:16, "For where you have envy and selfish ambition, there you find disorder and every evil practice." Your life and work environment do not need disorder and evil practice. Envy is jealousy and covetousness rolled into one. It is also equated biblically with murderous intent, stealing, and pride. It can consume you. Obviously, it is a quality to be contained and avoided. If you envy, you are not practicing love.

Love does not boast and is not proud. Boasting is its own reward. If you do something and brag about how wonderful you are, you have already received your reward, such as it is. If you try to take all the credit for the work of the team, you are displaying pride and selfishness, neither of which equates with, or can exist in conjunction with, love.

Verse 4 of this tightly packed passage is probably all we can focus on this week. The challenge is to work on developing a kind of love for others in your office that is active and focused on appreciating your co-workers—and showing it with kindness and patience. Next week we will continue with the focus passage in 1 Corinthians 13:4–8a.

Reflections

_____

_____

_____

_____

_____

_____

_____

_____

34

Love's Imperatives

LAST WEEK WE looked at verse 4 of 1 Corinthians 13:4–8a. This week let's focus on verse 5: "[Love] does not dishonor others, it is not self-seeking, it is not easily angered, it keeps no record of wrongs." This too is a powerful verse. Can you see how the principles can be applied to your office? Be honest—I'll bet some of you are already wishing that a certain person in your office would read this! Hopefully, no one else is reading it and thinking of you!

How do we "dishonor" someone? Usually it is through how we talk about them or their work. If a person is rather unusual in mannerisms or behavior, does not quite fit in with the crowd, or may be older and less than cool because of the way they talk or dress, we dishonor them, either to their face or behind their back, by our word choice, our tone, the snicker or roll of our eyes, or the implication of our words in relation to them. It does not take much effort to be guilty of dishonoring someone. Often this demeaning behavior is coupled with our own self-seeking desires, enabling us to put someone else down in subtle, but effective, ways. You know what I mean.

How easily are you angered? Are you aware of the triggers or hot buttons that are easily pushed to get you to lose your temper? Conversely, do you have a co-worker with a quick temper and know exactly how to get a reaction? We as fellow workers, and especially as Christians, should be self-aware and avoid deliberately provoking others. One of the most successful managers with whom I worked had a policy for himself. If something happened in the office that really angered him, if at all possible he would wait till the next day to address the situation. When I asked him about this, he explained that he wanted to make sure his actions were practical, correct, and not clouded by anger. He wanted to think through the events without emotion. He wanted to produce good, long-term results and be fair and just with his employees.

Anger manifested in temper-fueled outbursts is wasted energy, displaying limited coping skills and seldom, if ever, producing good results. It often requires more work to correct what is done in reactive anger than to wait and control your response. Be patient. Think. Develop control over your reactions and be slow to anger. How many times have you heard someone fume, "I will forgive, but I will never forget"? This is the modern way of "keeping a record of wrongs." There are any number of things that happen each day that could offend us. Mistakes happen. People say things. Sometimes, but not often, they apologize and seek to move along. Let it go. Whether or not they acknowledge their fault and seek forgiveness, forgive and move on. To do this, you must throw away that mental list. Remember that love is active and even proactive; this may be an area you need to develop as you strive to love others.

Let this little verse and its directives challenge you this week. Next week we will finish considering this beautiful and powerful passage from 1 Corinthians 13. I hope you have used these words as the backdrop for a close look at yourself and your working environment. You are the key to making relationships better in the office and setting a good example for others to follow.

Reflections

_____

_____

_____

_____

_____

35

Proactive Love

KNOW THAT MOST of you associate this passage in 1 Corinthians 13 with weddings, but I hope you have seen how powerful it can be when applied to you and your work setting and everyday life. It is a passage about relationships, and if love is your motivation you are on the right track. If you want to win over that difficult co-worker to being more open to suggestion, or to just being easier to get along with, try using the spiritual traits mentioned in these verses.

Verse 6 says, "Love does not delight in evil but rejoices with the truth." It is easy to agree with the first part of this little verse. No decent person would take pleasure in evil or look forward to some unwholesome outcome for another person—even if they did not like that individual. But the second part of this verse, while perhaps easily overlooked, has a lot of meaning and direction for us.

If love is active, we as Christians should not just sit by and let an injustice happen. Love compels us to intervene to the extent we can. We have an obligation to the truth, to justice. Nothing is worse than a group of people standing around doing nothing while aware that a crime is being committed against someone within their sight or hearing. Christians have an obligation to speak up, putting forward ideas and actions that promote the truth and a positive outcome.

If there is a situation at work in which we can see that someone is about to get into trouble, whether wittingly or unwittingly, it becomes our duty to speak up. Maybe we don't particularly like the person, or perhaps we feel they are due for a reality check with regard to their ego, but we should not sit gleefully by as they fall off the cliff. Quietly, lovingly, we can point out the potential problems their attitudes or actions are about to cause or call to their attention that their planned action is against policy. If they choose to ignore our well-intentioned advice, they have made a choice, and the result is their responsibility.

Your motivation in approaching that person should be active, selfless love. As we are reminded in verse 7, love "always protects, always trusts, always hopes, always perseveres." If your actions toward or on behalf of your fellow worker are motivated in this way, you are on the right track and are practicing active love. Verse 8 sums it up: "Love never fails." And verse 13 tells us that the greatest spiritual quality we can possess is love.

Let your challenge for the week be to apply love to every situation in your life, particularly as it pertains to the work environment and its dynamics. Test the truths Paul has shared in this jam-packed gem of a passage. Instead of harsh, negative words, speak with kindness, truth, and love to and about those around you. Seek to encourage and support your co-workers in positive ways. Actively love them, and you will be a witness to the love and mercy you have received from Jesus' atoning death and resurrection.

Reflections

_____

_____

_____

_____

_____

_____

_____

36

Standards for Wholesome Speech

NE OF THE benefits of working outside the home is that you get to interact with people on a regular basis. The group with whom you work becomes a part of your family in many ways. Sometimes an office grouping will be made up of people from many walks of life and very different backgrounds, and working there could present a cultural shock to you in many ways. We all feel pressured to join in, fit in, and become part of the office culture.

If you have come from a fairly conservative family and background, you may not be familiar with different manners of speaking by people from other backgrounds. In your office you may interact with someone who sees everything that happens from a sexualized context. They often make suggestive remarks or tell off-color jokes about others and verbalize thoughts or notice innuendos that would never have entered your head. Or there may be someone who laces everything they say with profanity. And what can we say about negative, demeaning, or mean-spirited remarks regarding race, gender, age, or any other characteristic?

If you are in an office, school or workplace with an environment that is polluted in any of these ways, you have my sympathy. No environment could be more uncomfortable. None of us likes to feel as though we don't fit in, but at the same time we need to identify and then abide by our own personal standards. That decision should be made ahead of time so that we will be prepared to confront the issue. The apostle Paul made it very clear in Ephesians 5:4 what our workday (and all other) speech should be like: "Nor should there be obscenity, foolish talk or coarse joking, which are out of place, but rather thanksgiving."

Paul provides further guidelines in Ephesians 4:29: "Do not let any unwholesome talk come out of your mouths, but only what is helpful for building others up according to their needs, that it may benefit those who listen." And again in verses 31–32, "Get rid of all bitterness, rage and anger, brawling and slander, along with every form of malice. Be kind and compassionate to one another, forgiving each other, just as in Christ God forgave you." Paul had earlier urged Christ's followers to speak the truth in love. We must, without anger or bitterness, find a way to indicate to our fellow workers that we do not want to hear, let alone participate in, off-color or derogatory comments. In time, with a loving manner and response, we may be able to win them over. Maybe we won't succeed in changing them, but we can and will be a witness that we do not intend to profane or demean others.

I find it interesting as I study the Bible that humankind has not changed and that the people of the first century had the same flaws as we do today.

Let your challenge for this week be to live out in the workplace Paul's teaching on wholesome speech. Pray actively for your working environment and for those whose speech standards are not of the highest caliber.

Reflections

_____

_____

_____

_____

_____

_____

_____

37

Self-Evaluation

W HAT KIND OF worker are you? Do you require a lot of guidance and hand holding to get motivated to start working? Are you often late for work or tempted to leave early? Do you devote a lot of time for personal phone calls, looking up items on line, or checking your social media and emails? What do you do when the boss leaves the office? Does your work slow down until she returns? Do you conceal mistakes? Do you help yourself to some free postage or office supplies?

The answers to these questions will reveal who you really are. If any were hard to answer, you need to do some digging into your innermost character.

For fun, let's see where you score:

(Score 5 points for "Never"; 4 points if you spend less than 10 minutes per day on the activity; 3 points for 10–30 minutes per day; and 1 point if you spend more than 30 minutes per day on any one of these activities.)

1. Talking/chatting about non-work-related items with fellow workers throughout the day. _____
2. Talking to kids, family members, or friends. _____
3. Emailing or texting regarding non-work-related matters. _____
4. Leaving the office on company time for personal errands/ matters. _____
5. Searching the web, magazines, etc., for personal matters, news items, etc. _____
6. Using office supplies or postage for personal use. _____
7. Stopping work when the boss leaves the area. _____
8. Gossiping about fellow workers or the bosses. _____

9. Making negative comments about the business or its policies. _____

10. Coming to work late or slipping out early. _____

The perfect score would, of course, be 50. I would say that a very good employee would score between 40 and 50 points. An average employee would score 30 to 40. No need to comment on those scoring below that. Do you realize that if you were to engage in just five of those listed activities for ten to twelve minutes each day, you would be taking an hour of production away from your employer?

Although we are not slaves today, we are workers. We are bound to our jobs and owe our employers diligent, careful, and hard work. If you read and heed the apostle's advice in Ephesians 6:5–8 and Colossians 3:22–25, you will be encouraged to obey your employer (and follow the office policies) with a sincere heart, whether or not you are being watched. I resonate with Paul's words of Colossians 3:23: "Whatever you do, work at it with all your heart, as working for the Lord, not for human masters."

What else needs to be said? Your challenge for this week is to see whether you can increase your point count.

Reflections

_____

_____

_____

_____

_____

38

Creation's Pinnacle

THE PURPOSE OF this weekly devotional book has been to encourage the busy working woman of today. That includes all of us. We live in a frenetic age. It is not my intent to wander into the political realm in my writing. The Bible should be our only guide; it provides all the answers we need for our lives today. I am convinced that in another twenty to thirty years those of you who are reading this book will have forgotten about the persons and events that seem so important within today's political arena. Politics is just not that important in the long run. The Bible and its words, on the other hand, are everlasting.

Let's look at an issue that is all around us, while trying to leave out the political ramifications. Let's consider what the Scriptures say about life and the people we are. As related in the opening chapters of Genesis, God created people, breathing life into the first man. All life is a creation of God, and human beings are the pinnacle of His creation. God created people for the purpose of entering into fellowship with Himself. If we accept that people are the highest form of creation, given the power to have dominion over all else in creation, we cannot help but conclude that all human life is precious.

You may have realized that I am introducing the touchy subject of abortion. There are many reasons we should try to convince any woman who is expecting to do everything possible to preserve the nascent life God has placed within her. Abortion should be and is a heart matter—not a political issue.

In Genesis 1:27 we see that God created humankind in His very own image. God used the same creation powers that He had used when he created the universe, and He is sovereign over all His creation. He also orchestrated the process for propagating and thus continuing the species. Each life is vital and has a divine purpose.

The argument has been that "it" (that often maligned and disregarded fetus) is not a person until birth. Let's see whether Scripture supports this premise. Two major prophets, Jeremiah and Isaiah, along with the apostle Paul, record that God knew them and had plans for them before they were born. Jeremiah 1:5 sums this up with the Lord speaking these words to Jeremiah: "'Before I formed you in the womb I knew you, before you were born I set you apart.'" God's setting apart the prophet (and by extension each of us) means that He had a purpose for Jeremiah from the very moment of his conception. That purpose, whatever it might be for any of us on an individual basis, still applies, and it means that there is a purpose at conception for each life.

If this were true of these men, it is true today for every child conceived. God has a plan for each of us. He knows us before we are born. He sees us, His purposeful creations. If in doubt, take the time to read David's poignant words in Psalm 139:13–16.

The challenge this week is vital and sensitive in nature. If you know a woman at work or in your circle of family or acquaintances who might be considering abortion, share these Scriptures with her. Encourage her in a loving way to first realize that she is precious in God's eyes and the worthy recipient of His love. Her developing child was conceived by God's plan, and He has a purpose for her, too. What a privilege it would be to help that little life find her purpose as a part of God's creation.

Reflections

_____

_____

_____

_____

_____

_____

39

Affordable Giving

RECENTLY HEARD Dr. Charles Stanley make a comment to the effect that when we get to heaven we will be judged not based on the things we have achieved or received in life but by what we have given to others. This makes sense. Yet on what endeavors do we spend most of our time? Achieving and acquiring . . . or giving?

Some of you may protest that you do not have enough resources yourself to give much to others. But, I don't see this principle as necessarily applying only, or even primarily, in the material sense. We all have the same number of hours in a day. All of us in the work environment have an opportunity to take a few minutes each day to, at the very least, acknowledge our fellow workers and offer a word of encouragement.

Sometimes it takes a real effort to speak to that particular individual in the office who is the most difficult to approach. We can find a million excuses—and they may be valid in themselves—to pass them by and avoid the inevitable complaint, shrug, or tacky remark the person is famous for delivering. After all, they are the least loved in the office for good reason, and you may want to avoid the negative vibes you know they can deliver.

Sometimes our own mood is "down," negative, or depressed. You may have had the morning from you-know-where getting the kids off to school, cleaning up the kitchen, locating misplaced keys, and arguing with your spouse over whose turn it is to pick up the cleaning or get the car into the shop. You hope someone else will cheer you up, and you would rather not get involved with those difficult people in the office.

Although you may not think you have much to give, to just offer a kind word or acknowledgment sends the powerful message that you see and value them—a form of giving that can mean a lot to another. Scripture calls on us to love our enemies and even pray for them. We are to do unto others what we would have them do for us. In John 13:35 Jesus commanded us to love one another *as He has loved us.* That is a pretty heady commandment, and one we had best not ignore!

What, we might ask, would be in it for us if we were to follow through with this? First of all, we would be obeying a commandment straight from Jesus. Further, the truth, counterintuitive as it may seem, is that when you give of yourself you forget yourself and your troubles and in doing so lift your own spirits. You rise above the mundane in your life.

It does not take much effort to be kind, and benefits will come to you. Proverbs 11:17 observes that "those who are kind benefit themselves, but the cruel bring ruin on themselves." You may not be a person who has been blessed with a lot of wealth to share, but each of us can cultivate the power to be kind, thoughtful, or even merely polite to those with whom we work. To share a moment of time to express a word of concern or encouragement may be all you have to offer at any given moment, but it can mean a lot to those with whom you work and will help you forget your own troubles.

Your challenge for this week should be clear. Find ways to devote a few moments of your time to encouraging or being kind to others around you this week.

Reflections

_____

_____

_____

_____

_____

_____

40

Numbering Our Days

AS I BECOME older, I'm noticing that I spend a lot of time reflecting on my time. I reflect on my time in the past and on how much I have seemed to waste, and on the time I might have left and how I can best use it. I would suppose that this is natural.

When you are younger, you do not think of time as a set commodity that can run out or be limited. There is just what I must do today or this week or what I may plan in the future. We humans tend to conceive of "time" as starting with ourselves and to consider ourselves unique; though our rational minds tell us otherwise, we presume in our life that we will live forever and perhaps even that what we are doing now is the most clever and creative of all historical achievements: no one can surpass us or compare favorably against us.

So it may come as a shock when we are asked about retirement. "What do you mean I should consider retirement? Why? I plan to just keep going. I have a lot more to accomplish. I have plenty of time . . . or do I?"

Each generation thinks of itself as the most special, the most gifted. But wait—that implies that there will be generations after me. Where does my generation fit in terms of the continuum of time? Will the next generations view me as I view those who have fairly recently preceded me? To me they were just a mist, an insignificant group comprised of old-fashioned and uninformed people who did not know or do what I am able to do today with my educational background and levels of expertise in technology and science.

Read Moses' words in Psalm 90 to get a feeling for eternity and the relentless, onrushing cycle of generations. "A thousand years in your sight are like a day that has just gone by, or like a watch in the night," the psalmist reflects wistfully in verse 4. And in verse 12 he asks the Lord to "teach us to number our days, that we may gain a heart of wisdom."

James 4:14 points out, "Why, you do not even know what will happen tomorrow. What is your life? You are a mist that appears for a little while and then vanishes." From Scripture we see that our life's appearance on this earthly stage is very short. We need to make the most of our time, to gain insight into what is really important for us to follow or pursue.

If our time here is so short, what is most important? What will happen after the passing of our generation? Where will we be? What will we be doing? How can we prepare? These questions lead us to the need to seek wisdom for our lives. We need to seek the eternal, to be conscious that our days are truly numbered. The ultimate phase of eternity waits at the end of our years here on earth. We spend so much time preparing for the transitions in this life, but we need to consider the ultimate destiny ahead for each of us—beginning with the critical first step of considering God's gift of His Son, Jesus, and its meaning for us.

This week, search your heart to clarify what you truly believe and in whom your trust and loyalty lie. You are living in eternity right now, and if Jesus is not part of your present life, if you have not fully accepted Him and invited him into your life, it is vital that you do so. If your time were to be "up" in human, worldly terms, and if you had not made that ultimate, all-in commitment, you would be entering eternity without Him. You must not put off a decision that can and will affect you throughout eternity, because no decision constitutes a default decision.

Reflections
_____

_____

_____

_____

41

Highs and Lows

HOPE YOU ARE in a career you love. You may not have started out to do the particular work you do today, but hopefully you have come to terms with your job and what you see as a career path. Careers and the working years can be long, and it is so much better if we look forward to going to work each day.

No matter how much you love your job or feel you have prepared for a particular field, there will be moments of discouragement. Contrary to common sense, we often become discouraged, and even depressed, following some significant achievement or accomplishment in our job. This up and down rollercoaster just doesn't make sense. We were successful. We accomplished a major goal. People were pleased and praised us, and yet in a matter of days we find ourselves down in the dumps.

I am sure all sorts of psychological and scientific explanations could be put forth, but the fact is that this kind of emotional fluctuation is human nature. When on a job "high" due to some successful effort, you are on the mountaintop. You want to stay there. You want to continue to bask in the glory of what you have accomplished. You do not want the good feelings to end. You want the praise to continue—after all, you deserve it.

Then reality sets in. The previous success is soon forgotten. The company wants more from you. New goals and projects become the focus. What are you going to do for us now?" becomes the question. Someone in the office, who is not particularly in your corner anyway, becomes critical, demanding, and even makes hurtful comments or insinuations. Your previous contributions are minimized. You are hurt. Discouraged. Your pride is wounded. You wonder why you work so hard if you are not going to be appreciated.

Relax. This is human nature. We all want to stay on the mountaintop of glory and bask in success. It is hard to face the reality that we have got to get back into the grind and face the new challenges put before us. Sometimes it is hard to move on, and we just wish we could crawl into a hole and die.

Don't go there! If you are already there, get up and get out. Get busy. Put the hurt and frustrations out of your mind. Try to focus on others. Look for ways to serve as you work together. Remain humble and avoid letting your pride control you. Depression is a snare that, once it gets a hold on you, is hard to shake. Even the prophet Elijah became depressed after performing great miracles against pagan priests. God was with him in a mighty way on Mt. Carmel. Yet criticism and threats by Queen Jezebel caused him to flee for his life and pray that he might die. He was ready to give up. God spoke to him in a quiet whisper and basically told him to get up and get busy. God gave him new tasks to do. He instilled in him renewed purpose and direction. You, too, have a purpose. There are tasks you need to do. People you need to help. Your life is not over until there is literally nothing left for you to do. As Paul enjoins us in 1 Thessalonians 5:16–18, "Rejoice always, pray continually, give thanks in all circumstances."

Joy and depression cannot occupy the same person at the same time. Strive for a joyful day. Pray for a joyful day. Give thanks for God's presence with you at all times and for the ability to spread joy to those around you.

Reflections

_____

_____

_____

_____

_____

42

No Time Like the Present

W HO KNOWS BUT that you have come to your place and position in life for such a time as this? This question was asked almost twenty-five hundred years ago to Queen Esther by her uncle, Mordecai, as she faced a serious challenge that carried the weight and survival of herself, her family, and her people who remained in Persia following the return of the exiles to Judah. The question is relevant for you today in the life and position you hold.

If you have never questioned why you are here and what purpose you serve, today is a good time to address the issue head on. Maybe you feel unimportant or suspect that you do not matter. If so, consider this. Your influence is like a series of concentric circles. Start with yourself in the middle—a little circle—and draw circles around you, intersecting with and overlapping yours, of those you influence. Your first circle would be your immediate family and the next, friends. Add one for co-workers and another for the various social groups with whom you have a connection due to your children's activities in school, sports events, clubs and organizations with which you are affiliated, and the like. Include s a circle for your church family and subgroups within that, and so on. Pretty soon you begin to see yourself as part of a much larger picture. You see that you are the small circle in a series of concentric circles representing those who are influenced by you. What you do, what you say, and how you act send out pulses and waves of influence that make this picture vibrate and move. You are powerful and important to those around you.

Then consider your interests and what causes you should support. There are needs all around you. Ask yourself in what capacity you can effectively serve others. Where can you be a help and inspiration to others? Where can your efforts relieve some need? There is a lot to be done, and you may be just the one to make a great difference in your family, office, community, or church.

Don't be afraid to step up. The same question expressed in Esther 4:14 should pierce our hearts and minds. Who knows but that you have been placed in your position to be the one to step up for such a time as this? Don't let the opportunity pass you by. Search for your purpose and find your voice to speak up to help those around you, whether by championing some important cause, showing kindness to someone, or just being a strong moral example. In all these activities seek to honor God and display His love, and you will be fulfilling your purpose.

Reflections

43

Your Unique Calling

ARLIER IN OUR weekly studies I mentioned several Old Testament women and the strong roles they played in the times they lived. Both the Old and the New Testaments reveal that Israelite/Jewish women tended to hold elevated places in society compared to the situation in the nations around them. This reflects attributes of our God and His plans for all humankind for eternity. We are told that in Christ there is no distinction, that all who believe will receive eternal life. In Galatians 3:28 Paul declared that "there is neither Jew nor Gentile, neither slave nor free, nor is there male and female, for you are all one in Christ Jesus."

I want us to look at some New Testament women and see what we can learn from their lives that might help us today. Timothy's mother, Eunice, and his grandmother, Lois, were both women of deep faith in God who took on themselves the role of teaching him Scripture—Timothy's father being a nonbeliever. Paul acknowledges their role in Timothy's life and faith. They were devout women who bequeathed to Timothy a foundation of faith and enabled him to become a leader who would bring many to a saving knowledge of Christ. See 2 Timothy 1:5; 3:14–15. You, too, as a woman of faith, can pass that faith along, not only to your children but also to those with whom you work, often by just being yourself and setting a Christian example of how to handle the workplace issues and problems you encounter each day.

There was also a group of women who served and supported the apostles and Jesus during His earthly ministry. These women are frequently named and referenced in the New Testament, and they played a significant role in Jesus' ministry. Several were wealthy and used their influence and resources to help advance the gospel. All four Gospels mention several of these women by name—especially in the context of Jesus' death and resurrection. See John 19:25–27 as an example. While the apostles were in hiding, the women took note of where Jesus' body was placed and made arrangements to attend to it, according to the custom of the day. Mary Magdalene, a woman with a shady past, was the first person to whom Jesus spoke after his resurrection. Read the story in John 20:10–18.

The book of Acts mentions several women. Lydia was a businesswoman of the day who made purple garments. If you research how purple was produced, you will realize that it involved a difficult, complex, and expensive process. She was an early convert and financial supporter of the Christian movement. Acts 12 and 16 record events in her life.

Whether you are a woman of means who can assist financially with many causes or one who serves others in various other ways, you are fulfilling the role you were called to play. Being blessed financially means that you have the opportunity to help provide for others in their times of need. If you have the ability to see a need and provide a service, that, too, is an important role. Your sensitivity to those who have a need in your work environment and your willingness to help them with some task or provide comfort or counseling may constitute the only Christian testimony they see. Such seemingly small steps have served to lead many to Christ. The bottom line is that believing women have an important and necessary role to play in all aspects of life, and all we need to do is prayerfully step up to offer ourselves.

Your challenge is to recognize and step into your role. Step up to the opportunities offered. Share a kind word, offer some service or encouragement, and live the life that reflects Christ and His love for all.

Reflections

44

From Faith into Action

A FRIEND RECENTLY SENT me a quote I think reflects a lot of wisdom: "Going to church doesn't make you a Christian any more than standing in a garage makes you a car."

Think about this for a minute. It makes sense. Becoming a Christian is an act of faith. This is the first step needed. However, as the biblical James so succinctly put it, faith without works is dead ("useless" in the NIV; James 2:20). If you are a Christian, you cannot sit still. You have a call (actually, a command) to active service with the gifts you have been given. If a car sits too long in a garage, it will have trouble running. It will still be a car but of no use to anyone until it has a tune-up and begins to move again.

So it is with the Christian life. The church provides opportunities for you to "move" (exercise) those talents with which you have been gifted and become the *who* and *what* you were designed to be—an awesome force of love and service for the Lord. Attending church regularly, developing a prayer life, and studying the Scriptures are important maintenance functions that will keep you in tune and attuned to God and those around you, that will provide the fuel you need. Don't forget that, once filled, the Christian needs to move to action.

Your workplace is filled with opportunities to put your talents to work. First, you set an example of an honest, hard-working employee. There is good advice in 1 Thessalonians 4:11b–12, where Paul tells each of us to "mind your own business and work with your hands, . . . so that your daily life may win the respect of outsiders and so that you will not be dependent on anybody." Proverbs 18:9 warns, "One who is slack in his work is brother to one who destroys." You owe it to yourself and to your employer to set the pace for diligent, honest effort throughout the workday.

Do you either stir the pot or serve to put a lid on things that are getting out of hand in the office? As Proverbs 26:20 reminds us, "Without wood a fire goes out; without a gossip a quarrel dies down." Jesus promised that peacemakers would be called the sons [children] of God. Peacemaking, the ministry of reconciliation, is a high and noble calling. Your talent may be to calm the forces of conflict, jealousy, and anger that fuel the gossipmongers in the office. If so, do all you can to keep your skill sharp and ready to use each day—there will be plenty of opportunities.

Your challenge is to keep your spiritual battery charged with faithful church attendance, study of the Scriptures, and the development of a sound prayer life. Then seek to use whatever talents you possess to promote peace and serve as a good example of Christian character in your office each day.

Reflections

45

The Friendship Tightrope

TARTING A NEW JOB? Moving into a new position or office? You naturally want to fit in. We all desire to be accepted, become popular, and have friends. We work a significant number of hours each day, and it is important to maintain friendly relationships at work.

Finding and keeping friends is a powerful motivation in our lives. We may not articulate this desire aloud, but the instinct resides within us to seek out people with whom we might nurture a friendship relationship. After all, we are social animals. Even the most timid person needs and seeks human connection.

However, the Bible has some words of caution as we eagerly seek friendship. Whom we choose to have as friends says a lot about us. Friends are usually a mirror of our own personality, and a friend can have a powerful influence on our lives. The Bible cautions us about selecting friends for these and many other important reasons. There may be some people we really should not cultivate as friends.

Proverbs contains numerous pearls of wisdom concerning friendship. Let me encourage you to read the first chapter in its entirety—in as many different translations as you can. The passage speaks to choosing your associations carefully.

I think that the author of Proverbs said it well, and I am not going to add comment. I have no doubt you will get the message from the plain words of the verses. Some examples further on in the book include Proverbs 13:20; 20:19; 22:24, and 28:7.

The New Testament contains words of advice on this subject as well. There are many, but let's look at a couple. In 1 Corinthians 5 Paul points out that we live in a world inhabited by unsaved persons. We cannot help but associate with people who do not share our convictions and moral values. It is our goal to win them to the Lord. As we interact with them, we are sharing our testimony. However, in verse 11 he cautions us to be discerning when associating with people who claim to be believers but exhibit the negative behaviors he explicitly lists. His concern was for the developing churches, but I would suggest that you look at this list and consider his advice when it comes to choosing friends: "But now I am writing to you that you must not associate with anyone who claims to be a brother or sister but is sexually immoral or greedy, an idolater or slanderer, a drunkard or swindler. Do not even eat with such people."

Let's look at Paul's advice to his young friend Timothy. Paul notes that with each passing year we must acknowledge that we are moving closer to the end times. Second Timothy 3:2–5 describes what people will be like in the last days. Listen to his words, below. Are you reminded of anyone you know? "People will be lovers of themselves, lovers of money, boastful, proud, abusive, disobedient to their parents, ungrateful, unholy, without love, unforgiving, slanderous, without self-control, brutal, not lovers of the good, treacherous, rash, conceited, lovers of pleasure rather than lovers of God—having a form of godliness but denying its power. Have nothing to do with such people." If any of your potential friends demonstrate any of these characteristics, I would heed Paul's advice and avoid them. *We must love and witness to them, certainly, but we must not allow them to influence us to the point that we become like them.*

Your challenge this week is a big one. Prayerfully consider your present group of friends and determine whether they are leading your closer to the Lord or away from Him. You may have some hard choices to make.

Reflections

_____

_____

_____

_____

_____

46

Prayer Power

O VER THESE PAST weeks we have mentioned a great number of situations and issues that regularly come up in a work environment from time to time. In every one prayer was suggested as one way to deal with the situation. The burning question is this: Do you really know what prayer is and what it can do? Do you take full advantage of the power of prayer as you face your daily issues?

We know that prayer is our method of communication with our heavenly Father. Think about this. Here you are, one of several billions of people on this planet, each of whom has the ability and invitation to speak to the Creator of the whole universe through prayer.

Does He hear? Each one of us on an immediate basis? In Psalm 139:4 David asserts that, "Before a word is on my tongue you, LORD, know it completely."

Does God care? Jesus said, "'If you then, though you are evil, know how to give good gifts to your children, how much more will your Father in heaven give good gifts to those who ask him!'" (Matthew 7:11).

Is there a particular stance in or approach to prayer that God will honor? If we come to God in prayer with wrong motives and a sinful heart that is separating us from a right relationship with God, He is not going to hear us. See Psalm 66:18 for confirmation of that reality, as well as the early verses in Isaiah 59. James 4:3 advises us that, "When you ask, you do not receive, because you ask with wrong motives, that you may spend what you get on your pleasures."

Further, we are taught in Scripture that our heart must be right when we approach God and that we need to be sure we are not holding a grudge against someone else. In Jesus' model prayer popularly known as the Lord's Prayer, we are taught to ask that God forgive our sins in the same way that we have forgiven others. Before asking for our own forgiveness, we need to proactively forgive and set right our relationships to others. See Matthew 6:12.

Matthew 6:5–8 contains beautiful instructions from Jesus himself. And Paul in 1 Thessalonians 5:17 instructs us to pray continually—or habitually. James 5:16 directs us to pray for one another and promises that the prayer of a righteous person will be powerful and effective. The list could go on as to the importance and power of regular prayer. There is no situation in an office setting that cannot be overcome with prayer.

We know that Jesus prayed often and alone. He valued His close relationship with His Father, and His example should teach us as well. There is strength in prayer far beyond our own limited resources. Paul writes about prayer and the power of the Holy Spirit, who is our advocate before the throne of God. And we know stories of great Christian prayer warriors who have regularly prayed and the powerful answers they have received. God is there, and He is listening. He is eternal, not bound by time or space. And He is all-powerful. What more can we ask?

Our challenge is to begin a consistent, habitual prayer life and to bring our issues, conflicts, desires, and questions to the Lord on a regular basis. At the conclusion of our prayers, we need to leave our concerns at His feet and let Him find the resolutions to our conflicts and concerns.

Reflections

_____

_____

_____

_____

_____

_____

47

God's Hot Buttons

THE TRUTHS OF the Bible are as relevant today as they were thousands of years ago. The reason is simple: God, who is eternal, gave the teachings—and His principles, like His character, are unchanging. Men and women have not changed in nature, either, from the first man's initial breath taken in Eden. Humans have always struggled against God's commands, and we certainly see that pattern continuing.

Let's unpack the principles in Proverbs 6:16–19 for today's woman. The passage begins with, "There are six things the LORD hates, seven that are detestable to him." That sentence alone should perk your interest. What are those things the Lord would find detestable (a very strong word!)?

Topping the list is "haughty eyes." The reference is to those proud and arrogant types who claim to know it all and do not want any instruction. They have little, if any, consideration for the opinions and worth of others.

How about "a lying tongue"? Do we see that in the workplace today? Coming to mind for me are half-truths, cover-ups, misleading statements, and failure to acknowledge the help others have provided.

Another issue is "hands that shed innocent blood." Isn't it a sad commentary on our life today that when we hear of a mass shooting it is often in a school or office setting? The anger, hatred, jealously, and selfishness that often build within a person can result in their taking a violent path to the point of attacking children or their fellow workers. We need to be alert to tensions and frustrations in co-workers and try to defuse the negative feelings as best we can.

Nearly every work setting has seen someone with "a heart that devises wicked schemes." This describes the conniver, the plotter, the manipulator, the spoon that is always stirring up trouble. Often it is hard to avoid their traps, but we can call them out in truth and gentleness. We need to avoid helping them by letting the stories, schemes, and gossip stop with us.

Fifth on the list is "feet that are quick to rush into evil." Every work setting has those who commit theft of time, office supplies, and money. Then there are those who are looking for shortcuts or ways to avoid carrying out the rules in a fair manner; or who discriminate against individuals in the office, customers, or students. They provide services for and respect those power brokers who can potentially offer favors to loyal followers. And there are those who cheat on taxes and find ways to scheme around other government regulations. So much in our acquisitive society centers around the self. Beware being drawn into any activity that is unfair or unlawful or that fails to treat everyone with the dignity and respect they intrinsically deserve.

One of the evils God most detests is injustice. This may be seen in everyday interactions at work. Unfair and unfounded complaints about a fellow worker, inaccurate descriptions of a co-worker's behavior or work product, repetition of gossip, and misleading comments of all kinds—all fall within the category of lies, and all promote injustice.

Rounding out the list comes "a man who stirs up dissension among brothers." Are you someone who stirs the pot or one who tries to keep the peace? Getting through life each day has enough challenges without people repeating gossip, raising "hot button" issues, or poking the bear. As Jesus said in Matthew 5:9, "Blessed are the peacemakers, for they will be called children of God." How much better the workplace would be if we were all peacemakers.

The challenge this week is to pick out one characteristic each day. Examine your own conduct and attitude in relation to each principle and work to turn any negative into a positive.

Reflections

_____

_____

_____

48

Workplace Provocations

WE HAVE ALL been taught to love others. We know we should love others as we love ourselves and treat them as we would like to be treated. In the workplace we may be with the same people for at least eight hours per day, and we begin to see clearly what we perceive as their flaws and imperfections. Have you ever wondered how others perceive you? What do you really look like to a fellow worker, student, or boss?

Scripture provides some measuring sticks for us to use in evaluating ourselves. Take Ephesians 4:31–32, for example: "Get rid of all bitterness, rage and anger, brawling and slander, along with every form of malice. Be kind and compassionate to one another, forgiving each other, just as in Christ God forgave you." Do fellow workers see any of these traits in you?

It is easy to pinpoint some of these negative characteristics in our fellow employees, but harder to spot them in ourselves. Before we begin to pat ourselves on the back for what we think is our superior behavior, we had better heed Paul's warning in Galatians 5:26: "Let us not become conceited, provoking and envying each other."

Paul provides some other suggestions for evaluating ourselves and for walking in a godless world. In Philippians 2:3–4 he instructs his readers to "do nothing out of selfish ambition or vain conceit. Rather, in humility value others above yourselves, not looking to your own interests but each of you to the interest of the others." In verse 14 he adds, "Do everything without grumbling or arguing." Do you see yourself valuing those around you? Do you help and encourage even when you just wish they would be quiet and go away? How do you treat the whiners and complainers?

Do you try to listen and redirect them toward a more positive path? Or do you join in and become part of the crowd?

It is a challenge and, frankly, a lot of hard work to get along with some in the workplace. It is easy to identify unfair job assignments and perceive lack of appreciation for the hard work you do. We see others who get more credit for their endeavors. We see favoritism, nepotism, cronyism, and many other unjust "isms." Nevertheless, we need to heed how we act so that, as Paul states in verse 15, we will be blameless and pure, without fault and shining like stars to those around us. Our goal at all times must be to reflect the goodness and glory of the Lord to those who are lost in the darkness around us. To value and respect others reflects the humble spirit so favored by the Lord.

Reflections

_____

_____

_____

_____

_____

_____

_____

_____

49

Office Pitfalls

AS I LOOK over my earlier reflections, I notice that I have quoted a number of verses in Galatians. Paul wrote this letter in a straightforward manner. His words are clear, concise, and direct. I like that.

In today's business world there are constant encounters with people and situations that try to pull us away from doing what we know in our hearts as Christians to be right. Paul recognized the same struggle in the lives and spiritual development of the Galatians. And he provided guidance that is relevant for us still today.

The apostle emphasizes the importance of showing love to people, of being gentle and kind. He repeats the command to love our neighbor as ourselves. I particularly appreciate Galatians 5:15, where he calls on his readers to stop biting and devouring each other, lest they destroy one another. Sage advice, and so true. What a peaceful working environment we would have if we could just get people to stop trying to destroy each other's reputations and productivity.

The spiritual person is constantly under attack from what Paul calls the sinful nature of humanity. Sinful acts, which can seem so pleasurable and desirable for a time, are a trap. In Galatians 6 Paul urges us to be gentle with someone who has been caught up in a sinful life, while at the same time being careful not to become drawn into the same behavior ourselves. We are to try to help others but must all the while remember that Satan is powerful and that our human nature is easily drawn in to the values that are popular in our society and culture. The way of the world is not the way of the Spirit.

Paul minces no words, explicitly listing activities we are to avoid. In Galatians 5:19–21 he specifies, "The acts of the sinful nature are obvious: sexual immorality, impurity and debauchery; idolatry and witchcraft; hatred, discord, jealousy, fits of rage, selfish ambition, dissensions, factions and envy; drunkenness, orgies, and the like. I warn you, as I did before, that those who live like this will not inherit the kingdom of God."

Your challenge this week is to evaluate your behavior toward others with whom you interact daily. Are you gentle and loving as you approach them? Are you being careful not to let them influence you in a negative way? Read again the list of specific pitfalls against which Paul cautions, and evaluate yourself as to which of them is most tempting in your life and how you can work to avoid these human and worldly urges. Perhaps you can take some time to read all of Galatians to better appreciate, within context, what Paul has to say.

Reflections

_____

_____

_____

_____

_____

_____

_____

_____

50

Reconciliation

IF YOUR WORKING environment includes a large staff of employees, you, no doubt, have at times found yourself caught in the middle between factions. Each faction may consist of only a small number of people or may center around a strong-willed individual, but their collective impact on the working environment can be great. These opposing alliances represent hostilities that may be comparable to the old feuds between leading families in rural America or those between past royal houses in Europe. No matter the size or type, these conflicting groups make working relationships and progress in an office difficult.

If you analyze the cause of the feud, you will generally find that it started with some minor squabble over some issue that is no longer relevant, though emotions on both sides continue to run high. The main characters are locked into their hatred of those on the other side. Whatever the root cause or original grievance, neither side will acknowledge any guilt or initiate any type of reconciliation. Forgiveness is evidently not an option.

Often those embroiled in an office feud are not even aware of the damage hatred, grudges, strife, and the like can do to one's body, mind, and spirit. Holding onto a grudge, lack of forgiveness, hatred, and a mean-spirited determination for revenge are all destructive to each individual's health and can deal a deadly blow to spiritual development. I am not a trained counselor or doctor, but I have observed these detrimental effects over the years in people who refuse to forgive, preferring to continue nursing a grudge.

Fortunately, Scripture provides some advice. Jesus clearly instructed us in His model prayer (Matthew 6:12) that we may ask to be forgiven only to the extent that we forgive others; if we fail to forgive, we cannot expect to be absolved of our sins. Jesus also instructed that if we are holding something against anyone, we are to lay aside our offering to the Lord and go and seek reconciliation before making the offering (Matthew 5:24). In our contemporary

parlance, we might say that we should not let another moment
go by without trying to make peace with anyone with whom an
offense has taken place in either direction. We may start by asking
for forgiveness or offering to forgive. It might be a matter of our
offering some type of restitution to someone we have wronged.
Whatever it takes, do not hold onto that burden. Do not let yourself
dwell on thoughts of hatred or revenge. Instead, make peace. Then
go and pray, worship, and serve.

Although we have looked at forgiveness in the context of a
work setting, the act is even more important in terms of those family grudges that often develop. Counterintuitive as this may seem,
family relationships are often the most dicey. So many emotions
are at play. It follows that family disputes and grudges can be the
most hurtful and destructive. We all know families that have been
torn apart, with one group ostracizing the other for some trivial
reason. I cannot think of anything more tragic than relatives who
will not talk to one another.

The challenge this week extends beyond work to all aspects
of your life. If you are carrying a grudge of any kind against any
person or group, pray for the strength of character to initiate a
reconciliation of some kind. Unburden yourself and make amends.
Your walk will be lighter, your health will improve, and you will
be following the Lord's commands to love.

Reflections

_____

_____

_____

_____

51

Plans and Priorities

HOW FAR AHEAD do you plan? I worked with a friend who taught me a lot about planning. He had a two-year plan, a five-year plan, and a general ten-year goal. At the time I met him I was doing well to plan for one day at a time.

Planning and worrying are not the same. Planning, to me, takes the worry out of life and helps to adequately and effectively prepare for the future. Planning is a matter of setting and following priorities.

We hear a lot about planning for the future, planning for retirement, planning to pay for your children's college, planning long-range goals for our business, and so on. What type of planning should you be doing as a Christian?

God had a plan, both for the world and for you personally, from the very beginning. If you study Scripture and look back through history, you can see His plans at work. He knew from the very beginning that one day He would send His Son to redeem humanity. He has promised that He will complete His master plan for human history with Jesus' return and the final judgment of humankind.

Have you thought about your life and the plans He has for you? Just as God told His prophet in Jeremiah 1:5, "'Before I formed you in the womb I knew you,'" so it is with each of us. God knows us and calls us individually to some purpose. In Jeremiah 29:11 we read, "'For I know the plans I have for you,' declares the LORD, 'plans to prosper you and not to harm you, plans to give you hope and a future.'"

God has plans and has revealed them, but what about your plans? Do they include a time for yourself and the Lord each day? Do they center too much on work and not enough on yourself and your time with your family and friends? Do your weekends include time for worship? Do you plan for your legacy to your children to be one that actively reflects the living Savior in your life?

As we go about our daily activities that include going to work and making a living, we need to give consideration to what is next.

What will be important through eternity? We need to expand our plans in the present to include the eternal life that is already now within each of us.

It is so easy to fall into the trap of centering our lives around our work. Work gives us accountabilities and tasks in a structured, organized way that makes sense in the world in which we live. Everyone understands the demands of work. Employment is important, but our working life should not be the center of our existence. Work should be an important component of our lives, but it should not be viewed as the personification of who we are. We are God's creation, and He has made us for a relationship with Himself. He truly values us and our time with Him. Individually, we need to get to know Him through Bible study, prayer, and striving to lead a life that reflects Him and His goodness. We have a responsibility to teach our children about Him and His plans for us. We have a duty and responsibility to support His church and spread the good news to others.

Your challenge this week is to investigate in your life the work you are doing that will have a lasting impact on you and those around you. Think of all the time you put in to planning for things like work and vacations and scheduling children's sports and social events, routine appointments, and the like. Then think about the time you give to the Lord. Once you have evaluated your use of your time, reprioritize, if necessary, to make sure the spiritual things are first. Then see how much lighter and easier it will be to handle all the other accountabilities demanded of you.

Reflections

_____

_____

_____

52

The Changeless One

THE WORKPLACES AND office environments we have traditionally known are changing. More and more people are working from home and interacting with fellow employees by computer. Many things today are changing. Our lives are moving at a hectic pace that continues to accelerate. These developments and others were predicted centuries ago. Wise scholars say, and I believe Scripture reveals, that we are approaching the end time.

The end of time is another subject—one we could stand to study in detail. However, my point here is that change is constant and inevitable. In the work environment policies, personnel, job assignments, technology, goals, and ownership of businesses— these and other factors can seem to be in a continuous state of flux, with each change instilling for a time tension and insecurity. All of this fluctuation causes chronic stress in our lives. Job uncertainty, along with changes in family life and schedules, all contribute to anxiety, sleepless nights, and worry.

We deal with change in different ways. Most people would say they really do not like change. There is comfort in maintaining a predictable status quo. But life, particularly in this fast-paced technological world, is not going to stay the same.

One reality does not change, and we can take tremendous comfort in it. God is unchanging and eternal. The prophet in Isaiah 9:6–7 speaks to this, and it is hard for our minds to comprehend. God is the same today as He was at the moment He created the universe, and He is available to us on a personal level as God the Father. One of the most amazing things about God is that He loves us—so much so that His Word declares that He *is* love (1 John 4:8). He cares achingly and infinitely about what happens to us and what affects us. His love, care, and provision for us are never ending. From before creation His plan was for each of us to be in a relationship with Him.

Isaiah 40:8 proclaims that the Word of the Lord will stand forever. And in 2 Timothy 3:16–17 Paul speaks to Timothy about the importance and usefulness of Scripture, which the apostle refers to as God-breathed. What is Scripture? It is God's Word to us, and it can therefore be counted upon to be true, eternal, and useful in every aspect of our lives. As such it begs to be read and committed to memory. The Bible not only reveals God's direct message to us but provides a constant, true North Star to guide all of our life and work.

If you are facing seemingly unending changes in your life and work, don't fear. Don't feel overwhelmed or give up. The everlasting God has provided the strength and ability for you to cope on the basis of your faith in God's eternal Son, Jesus. He has provided the power of the Holy Spirit to be with you as a daily companion. The apostle Paul summed this up in the poignantly beautiful words of Romans 8:38–39: "For I am convinced that neither death nor life, neither angels nor demons, neither the present nor the future, nor any powers, neither height nor depth, nor anything else in all creation, will be able to separate us from the love of God that is in Christ Jesus our Lord."

Now go into the office with confidence that you will be able to handle anything and everything that comes your way.

Reflections

_____

_____

_____

_____

_____

Afterword

WE HAVE COME to the end of a year. I commend you for taking the time each week to read and share in some thoughts and suggestions that were designed to encourage and celebrate the working woman. All women work in one way or another, of course. I look at my own daughter, who is a working professional who is parenting her own small daughter, and I see the cycle I experienced being repeated, though with even more demands on her time. I know that I did not take the time I should have to study Scripture, though I did make church attendance and church-related activities a priority because I knew that a solid foundation would be important to her for the future. I am so proud today to see my daughter and her husband actively engaged in church and taking their daughter with them. We have both been blessed with supportive husbands who are also active Christians. My prayer for all women would be that you will choose carefully who you partner with because it will make all the difference in your life and Christian walk.

As we come to the conclusion of this year of study, I wondered how I could sum up all of the suggestions and observations that I feel came from the Lord as I wrote this. Looking back, I acknowledge that I often lacked the time to cook as much as I would have liked. I often looked for things I could throw together into a crockpot, but I also enjoyed recipes and collected many over the years. What follows is a simple recipe you might consider using in your workplace setting to bring joy to your life and to others around us.

Preparation: To start any cooking project, you must prepare the vessel: your own heart. If your heart is right with the Lord, you will be set for eternity, and all that comes from that vessel will be good and lasting. So start by choosing Jesus as Savior and Lord. The vessel will then be filled by the Holy Spirit, with room enough for all that is good and pure to be included. Anything that seeks to defile the pure vessel can be cast aside with the help of the Holy Spirit.

Next, generously add the ingredients of love, compassion, kindness, humility, gentleness, forgiveness, self-control, goodness, honesty, loyalty, and joy. Lots of joy! Blend each of these with patience and prayer, remembering that our timing is not necessarily the Lord's.

Let each of these characteristics simmer in your vessel for as long as it takes to fully develop and set firmly in your life. In all things strive to live closer to the Lord each day, to produce fruit that will glorify and reveal Him to others. Consume all of these ingredients on a regular basis to increase your wisdom and help you to grow in knowledge and understanding. Share them with those around you. As you do, He will greatly multiply your joy and give you peace.

Although life and work will always present challenges, there is no challenge you cannot overcome with the Lord's help and Spirit's guidance in your life. Help is just a prayer away. May the grace, joy, and peace of our Lord Jesus Christ be with you.